Witness Lee

Basic Lessons on Life

Living Stream Ministry
Anaheim, California • www.lsm.org

First Edition, June 1993.

ISBN 978-0-87083-729-6

Published by

Living Stream Ministry
2431 W. La Palma Ave., Anaheim, CA 92801 U.S.A.
P. O. Box 2121, Anaheim, CA 92814 U.S.A.

Printed in Australia

14 15 16 17 18 19 / 12 11 10 9 8 7 6

CONTENTS

PREFACE

These basic lessons on life were given by Brother Witness Lee from February through November 1979, in Anaheim, California. They were given to the elders and co-workers in Southern California for the purpose of training the saints.

THE CREATION OF MAN

Scripture Reading: Gen. 1:26-27; 2:7-9; Prov. 20:27; 1 Thes. 5:23

OUTLINE

  I. The Creator—the Triune God.
 II. In God's image—Col. 1:15; 2 Cor. 4:4.
III. After God's likeness—Rom. 5:14.
 IV. With the dust for the body that man may exist.
  V. With the breath of life for a spirit that man may receive God—Prov. 20:27; John 4:24; Rom. 8:16.
 VI. God breathing the breath of life into man.
VII. To produce the soul so that man may live through the mind, emotion, and will.
VIII. The intention of God's creation of man.
 IX. Putting man before the tree of life, indicating that God wanted man to receive Him as life.
  X. Man being created as a vessel to receive and contain God.

This series of brief messages on life and service are being given for the purpose of training the saints. You need to pray much to get yourself into these messages, and even to get these messages into you. Merely to repeat what is here in black and white will be a kind of dead speaking of knowledge according to the dead letter. These messages may be considered as groceries, which you need to cook in a living way through much, much prayer. You have to pray yourself into the message, pray yourself into a burden, and pray that the message will become your personal message in a living way. These are just the materials, but you have to cook them. You have to labor on all these points, and you have to pray until you yourself get into these messages, making them your own messages. Then you will speak not my message but your message, and you will speak out from your being with much exercise of your spirit. Then whatever you speak will be living, will be personal, and will be with the living impact. I do hope that we will not carry out this training in a light way but in a way full of prayer, full of the Spirit, and full of life.

In this first lesson on life, we want to speak about the creation of man. We need to read all the verses cited in the Scripture Reading above and be impressed with the main points of these verses.

I. THE CREATOR—THE TRIUNE GOD

The Creator of man is the Triune God—the Father, the Son, and the Spirit. Man's creation was wrapped up with the Divine Trinity. It was not merely God who created man, but it was the Triune God—the Father, the Son, and the Spirit. This is based upon Genesis 1:26, which says, "God said, Let Us make man in Our image." Here the plural pronouns *Us* and *Our* are used, indicating that the very God who intended to create man is triune—the Father, the Son, and the Spirit. According to Genesis 1:26, it seems that before God came in to create man, the Triune God had a kind of "Godhead conference," a kind of conference among the Trinity, to make a decision about how to create man in His image and according to His likeness. The decision to create man was made by the Triune God, indicating that the creation of man was for the purpose of the Triune

God. The trinity of the Godhead is not for theological doctrine but for the dispensing of God Himself into man according to His divine economy. Thus, at the very beginning when God intended to create man, God decided to do so in His Trinity. This is why He said, "Let *Us* make man in *Our* image." God's intention in creating man was to carry out His economy for His dispensing of Himself into man.

II. IN GOD'S IMAGE

Colossians 1:15 says that the beloved Son of God is the image of the invisible God, and 2 Corinthians 4:4 says that Christ is the image of God. God decided in His Godhead to create man in His image, and the image of God according to the Bible is just Christ. This image is not a physical form, but it is the expression of what God is in all His attributes and virtues. All God's attributes and virtues are invisible. These are the constituents of God. God is full of invisible attributes and virtues. Christ is the expression of all that God is in His attributes and virtues, and this expression is the image. Thus, the image of God is the expression of God in all that He is.

We have to point out to people that the image of God does not mean a kind of a figure, a kind of an image, for people to worship, but it means the very expression of what God is. God created man in His image. This means that God made man to have the attributes and virtues that He has. When God created man, He created him in His image, according to His attributes and virtues, so that man can express Him through these attributes and virtues. For example, God has love, and God loves. God also created man that man may have love and that man may love. God has wisdom and God has His purpose, so God made man also to have wisdom and to have a purpose. God can think, God can consider, God can love, God can like and dislike, God can make choices, God can have intentions, and God can make decisions. God created man in the same way so that man could express God. What man has, however, is only the image of God's attributes and virtues but not the reality. Man must receive God as his life and content, and then God with His attributes and virtues will fill up man to become the reality of man's attributes and virtues.

Man was made in the image of God, which is Christ. This indicates that man was made for Christ to enter into man so that He could occupy man and use man as His vessel to express Himself. Man is a container. A container is always made in the form of the thing that it is going to contain. Suppose the thing that is needed to be contained is square. Then you make a square container. If the thing that is to be contained is round, then you make the container round. The container is made in the image of its contents. Man was made by God in the image of God, Christ, with the purpose that one day man would be taken over by Christ and filled up with Christ so that man would be Christ's container and Christ would be man's content.

we only have the shape (avocado container), not the reality (real avocado).

III. AFTER GOD'S LIKENESS

God's image is His inward being. God's likeness is His outward form. Inwardly, God has His being with all the attributes and the virtues, and outwardly, God has a likeness. On the one hand, God is invisible. Since God is invisible, how could God have a likeness? This is something very hard for us human beings to understand and to explain. God appeared to Abraham in Genesis 18 in the likeness of a man. We cannot say that God was invisible in Genesis 18 and that He did not have a likeness. God appeared to Abraham in a visible way with man's likeness. Genesis 18 shows that God has man's likeness. Man's likeness is after God's likeness. We human beings have a physical body, and this is our likeness. We also have our inner being. In the same way, God has His inner being and also His likeness. Man's outward body was created after the likeness of God. Before God was incarnated to be a man, He appeared to Abraham in the form of a man. The form of man is the form of God, for man was created after the likeness of God.

IV. WITH THE DUST FOR THE BODY THAT MAN MAY EXIST

Genesis 2:7 says that God formed a body for man with the dust of the ground. The physical body is for man's existence. Without such a physical body formed with the dust, man cannot exist. When man's body dies, the man dies, so man's existence is altogether dependent upon his physical body.

we're dependant on life. If we ever want to do anything, to be alive is the first criteria.

V. WITH THE BREATH OF LIFE FOR A SPIRIT
THAT MAN MAY RECEIVE GOD

God created man with the breath of life for a spirit that man may receive God. This is also recorded in Genesis 2:7. After God formed man with the dust of the ground to give him a physical body, God breathed the breath of life into the nostrils of man. The Hebrew word for *breath* in Genesis 2:7 is translated as "spirit" in Proverbs 20:27. Proverbs 20:27 says, "The spirit of man is the lamp of Jehovah." This is a strong proof that the breath of life God breathed into man's body was eventually the spirit of man.

Our body of dust is a physical organ, and our spirit of the breath of life is a spiritual organ. We have a body of dust as our physical organ to contact the outward, physical world; we also have the spirit that comes from the breath of life as our inward, spiritual organ so that we can contact God in the spiritual world. Thus, it is clear that the man created by God has two organs: the body formed with dust and the spirit that came from the breath of life.

Here we need to point out that the breath of life breathed into man at his creation should not be considered as something of God's eternal life. When God breathed the breath of life into man, He did not put His eternal life into man. The breath of life was not the eternal life, because God's intention was that man would exercise his own free will to choose God's eternal life. Because of this, God surely would not put His eternal life into man just by His own will, His own decision, without letting man exercise man's own will, even man's free will, to choose the divine life. According to His divine principle, God would let man exercise his own free will to choose God and take God as his life. This life is the eternal life, which man did not have at the time of his creation.

Another proof that man did not have God's eternal life when he was created is that after man ate the tree of the knowledge of good and evil, God closed the way to the tree of life lest man partake of the tree of life and live forever with his evil nature (Gen. 3:22-24). This proves that at the beginning when man was created, man did not have the life of God. What he had was the breath of life getting into him and becoming his human spirit, which is the organ for him to receive God into him as the eternal life. We must be clear about this.

According to the Bible, man was never able to receive the eternal life of God until the Lord Jesus came and died on the cross to accomplish redemption for us, thus opening the way for us to contact God as the tree of life. After Christ's death and resurrection, man could believe in the Lord Jesus and receive Him as the eternal life. Before Christ's death and resurrection, man could not have the life of God.

VI. GOD BREATHING
THE BREATH OF LIFE INTO MAN

God created man with the breath of life so that man might have a spirit as a kind of receptacle to receive God.

VII. TO PRODUCE THE SOUL
SO THAT MAN MAY LIVE
THROUGH THE MIND, EMOTION, AND WILL

The producing of man's soul is also recorded in Genesis 2:7. Genesis 2:7 says that when the breath of life was breathed into the nostrils of the body of man, man became a living soul. God used two kinds of materials—the dust for making man's body and the breath of life for producing man's spirit. When these two things came together, right away man became a living soul. This means that the soul is the issue of the breath of life getting into the physical body of man.

It is clear that man was made in three parts: the outward body, the inward spirit, and the soul as the very being of man. This is why 1 Thessalonians 5:23 says that our whole being is composed of our spirit, soul, and body. We are a tripartite man. The soul is our being with our body as the outward organ and with our spirit as the inward organ. The soul as our being is composed of the mind, emotion, and will. This is according to the revelation of the Bible. The Bible shows us that in our soul we have our mind to think, to consider things (Psa. 13:2), we have our emotion to love and to hate (1 Sam. 18:1; 2 Sam. 5:8), to like and to dislike things (Isa. 61:10; Psa. 86:4), and we also have our will to make decisions, to make choices (Job 7:15; 6:7; 1 Chron. 22:19). These are the functions of the soul.

VIII. THE INTENTION
OF GOD'S CREATION OF MAN

The intention of God's creation of man is that man may understand God's desire with his mind, like God's desire with his emotion, choose to take, to receive, God with his will, and eventually exercise his spirit to receive God as his life. God created a mind for man. By this mind man may understand God's desire. God also created man with an emotion. By this emotion man may like God's desire. God created man with a free will, and man may exercise this free will to choose, to make a decision, to take and to receive God into him as his life. Eventually, man may exercise his spirit to receive God as his life. This is the intention of God in His creation of man.

God created man in a way that was good for man to take God, to receive God, into man as his life. Man was created by God with a mind, an emotion, and a will and also with a spirit in the center of man's being as a receptacle for him to receive God. Thus, by his mind man can understand what God wants; by his emotion man can like, can love, can prefer, what God wants; and by his free will man can make a decision to choose God, to take God. Furthermore, man has a spirit as an organ, even a receptacle, to receive God into him as his life. This is God's intention in His creation of man.

IX. PUTTING MAN BEFORE THE TREE OF LIFE,
INDICATING THAT GOD WANTED MAN
TO RECEIVE HIM AS LIFE

God put man before the tree of life, indicating that God wanted man to receive Him as life. We have to see that at the very beginning, God had no intention to ask man to keep any law, to do anything good, or to bear any kind of burden. At the very beginning, right after God created man, God only put man in front of the tree of life. This indicated that God wanted man to receive Him as life, signified by the tree of life. God also warned man that he should be careful about his eating. Of course, what man did was altogether up to his own free will. What he chose to eat was up to him. But God's desire was that man would choose the tree of life, which means that man would choose God as life.

X. MAN BEING CREATED AS A VESSEL
TO RECEIVE AND CONTAIN GOD

Man was created as a vessel to receive and contain God. This is fully revealed in Romans 9:21 and 23 and 2 Corinthians 4:7. In Romans 9 we are told that God is a potter, and we are the clay. The Potter made the clay vessels, and He made us vessels of mercy, vessels unto honor, and even vessels unto glory. Our being vessels to contain God is not because we are so good and preferable to God; it is altogether a matter of God's mercy. God had mercy upon us, and He wanted us to be His vessels, so we are the vessels of mercy. We are vessels unto honor because we contain the God of honor. Eventually, we all will be filled with God's glory and glorified in the glory of God to become the vessels unto glory. Thus, God created us as vessels—vessels of mercy, vessels unto honor, and vessels unto glory to contain Him.

We must see that God's creation is to make us vessels to contain Him. We must stress this one point in this lesson—that man was made a vessel with a human spirit as a receptacle to receive God. This is the first lesson concerning life in our training. We have to make it so clear and so impressive to all the trainees that the creation of man was just to make man as a vessel with a receptacle, that is, our spirit, to receive God into us as our life.

A VESSEL OF GOD

Scripture Reading: Gen. 2:7-9, 15-17; Rom. 9:21, 23; 2 Cor. 4:7;
John 1:11-12; Col. 2:6

OUTLINE

I. With a spirit as the receptacle to receive God:
   A. The human spirit being very close to God the Spirit.
   B. The human spirit being able to contact God and to be one with Him—John 4:24; Rom. 8:16.
II. With a mind to understand God—Luke 24:45; Rom. 12:2.
III. With an emotion to love God—Matt. 22:37.
IV. With a will to choose God:
   A. Two trees, indicating two wills, two sources, and two possibilities for man to choose.
   B. Being charged to eat the right tree, indicating that God created for man a free will and that God wanted man to exercise his free will to choose Him.
V. God's prohibiting man from eating the tree of knowledge indicating that God wanted man to receive Him as life by enjoying Him—John 1:11-12; Col. 2:6.
VI. Man needing to be God's vessel to contain Him—Eph. 3:17a.

Focus: The focus of this lesson should be man being God's container.

In this lesson we want to see that the man created by God is a vessel of God.

I. WITH A SPIRIT
AS THE RECEPTACLE TO RECEIVE GOD

God's intention in making man is to have a vessel that can contain Him and express Him. In this lesson we want to stress this one crucial point—the man created by God is a vessel. Among many Christians this concept is absent. Many Christians think that man should be used by God as an instrument. The highest thought they have is that man should be God's servant. But the thought of man being a vessel of God is not with them, because there is not such a thought in our human mentality.

In God's thought man is just a container, not a means or an instrument. Unless man can be a vessel, a container to contain God and to be filled up with God, man can never be used by God to fulfill His purpose. Balaam, the Gentile prophet, was someone used by God, but in a very, very negative way. This is because he was a prophet but he did not become a vessel to contain God. He was not a container of God.

In Romans 9:21 and 23 Paul tells us that God's creation of man was just to produce, to create, man as a vessel to fulfill God's purpose. God created man as a vessel to contain Him just as a potter makes a vessel of clay to contain something. Second Corinthians 4:7 also conveys this thought. The apostle Paul considered himself as an earthen vessel to contain a treasure, and the treasure is just Christ, the very God. Thus, in Romans 9 and 2 Corinthians 4 we can see a clear revelation that man was created by God to be His vessel to contain Him.

As a container to contain God, man needs a receptacle to receive God, and this is the unique difference between God's creation of man and His creation of other things. God did not give any other created thing a spirit except man. According to Genesis 2:7, God created man with the dust to form a body. Then He breathed the breath of life into man's nostrils, and man became a living soul. Genesis 2:7 shows us a picture of man as a vessel made by God.

There is the need of a receptacle within man to receive and

contain God. Today's radio has an outward box and an inward receiver to receive the invisible radio waves. Genesis 2:7 shows us that man has an outward body made with dust, and an inward receptacle, an inward receiver, produced by God's breath of life. This inward receiver is the spirit of man.

A. The Human Spirit Being
Very Close to God the Spirit

The human spirit is very close to God the Spirit. Many Bible readers mistakenly think that the breath of life breathed into the nostrils of the dusty man was the life of God. They consider that at the time of creation, God imparted His life into man's earthen body. They do not see the difference between God's breathing the breath of life into man in Genesis 2:7 and the Lord Jesus' breathing the Holy Spirit into the disciples in John 20:22. When the Lord Jesus breathed the Spirit of God into the disciples, the eternal life entered into the disciples. But when God breathed the breath of life into the dusty body of man, that breath of life became man's human spirit.

Two principles do not allow us to say that God's life entered into man at his creation when God's breath of life was breathed into him. The first principle is that of man's free will. If God had put His eternal life into man at his creation, there would have been no need for man to exercise his free will. This would mean that God's creation accomplished His purpose without the exercise of man's will. This is against the divine principle of God giving man a free will.

Furthermore, according to the whole Bible, it is not only against the divine principle of man's free will but also against God's economy to say that man received God's eternal life at his creation. The whole Bible shows us that after God's creation, God wanted man to choose Him, so He put man in front of the tree of life, expecting that man would freely choose to receive God into him as life. It would be against His economy for God to put His life into man at the creation of man.

After the fall of man, God closed the way to the tree of life. According to the revelation at the end of Genesis 3, God closed the way to the tree of life so that fallen man would not live forever with his sinful nature (vv. 22-24). This shows us that man did not have the eternal life of God at the time of creation. Actually, man could not receive God's eternal life until the Lord Jesus passed through death and resurrection to accomplish redemption to solve the problem of sin for man and to release the eternal life of God.

Some wrongly say that man received the life of God at his creation based upon Luke 3:38, which says that Adam was the son of God. They maintain that Adam must have had the life of God; otherwise, he could not have been a son of God. But the angels are also called the sons of God (Job 1:6; 38:7). This does not mean that the angels have God's divine life with God's divine nature. In the Bible the word *son* has at least two meanings. One meaning is that a son is one who was born of the Father by the Father's life with the Father's nature. The second meaning is that a son is one who was created by God. Because Adam and the angels were created by God, they are called sons of God. God was their origin. Even adopted sons can be called sons of their adopted father, but they do not have his life and nature. Adam was considered the son of God because he was created by God, even as the heathen poets considered all mankind to be the offspring of God (Acts 17:28). Mankind was only created by God, not regenerated of Him. This is absolutely and intrinsically different from the believers in Christ being the sons of God. They have been born, regenerated, of God and possess God's life and nature (John 1:12-13; 3:16; 2 Pet. 1:4).

Although man did not receive God's life at his creation, he was created with a human spirit, which came from God's breath of life. Thus, although the human spirit is not the Spirit of God or the divine life of God, it is very close to the Spirit of God. This is why the human spirit can receive God the Spirit. A substance like copper has the ability to receive electricity, but wood or paper does not. Between the electricity and the copper there is no insulation but rather a kind of transmission. Likewise, between God the Spirit and our human spirit there is a kind of transmission; there is no insulation. But between our physical body and the Spirit of God or between our psychological being and the Spirit of God there is a kind of insulation; there is no transmission. Because the human spirit comes out of God's breath of life, our human spirit is very close to God the

Spirit. We have to stress this because this will lay a good foundation for the following lessons on life. We cannot help people to go on in life if we miss this very crucial point.

B. The Human Spirit Being Able
to Contact God and to Be One with Him

Because our human spirit is close to God, and there is a transmission between God the Spirit and our human spirit, our human spirit is able to contact God and to be one with God. John 4:24, which says that God is Spirit and those who worship Him must worship Him in spirit, proves that our spirit is able to contact God. Romans 8:16 says that the Spirit witnesses with our spirit. This verse uses the preposition *with*. This means that God's Spirit is one with our spirit. This little word *with* is very precious, indicating that now our spirit is one with God's Spirit. We need to stress these points again and again, especially with the new ones. The new ones who have come into the church life in the last two years need this kind of help.

II. WITH A MIND TO UNDERSTAND GOD

Man was made not only with a spirit but also with a mind to understand God (Luke 24:45; Rom. 12:2). To contact God, to receive God, and to contain God are one thing, but to understand God is another thing. We have a spirit to receive God, but we also have a soul, a psuche. In referring to people, the Bible calls them souls (Exo. 1:5, lit.; Acts 2:41). Every person is a soul. We are a psychological being, a soul, with the faculty of understanding. God created man with a mind, a part of the soul, so that man could understand God. The understanding is the function of the mind. Luke 24:45 says that the Lord opened the mind of the disciples to understand the Scriptures. This is a very good verse proving that we need to understand God.

III. WITH AN EMOTION TO LOVE GOD

Man was also created with an emotion to love God (Matt. 22:37). The Bible shows that in our psychological being, besides the mind as the understanding organ, there is also the emotion as the loving organ. Matthew 22:37 says that we should love the Lord our God with all our heart and all our mind. The

mind is also a part of the heart, but it is separately mentioned
in this verse. Since the mind is separately mentioned here,
surely this indicates that the heart in this verse must refer to
the loving function of the heart, that is, the emotion. After we
receive God, we have to understand Him. After we understand
Him, surely we have to appreciate Him, like Him, love Him,
and treasure Him. Thus, an emotion, the loving function of our
heart, was also prepared for us by God.

IV. WITH A WILL TO CHOOSE GOD

Man was created with a will to choose God. Without his
will, man would have no choice, no decision, no direction, and
no goal. Thus, God created a strong choosing organ for man. In
our psychological being, our will is the strongest part. Even
after the fall of man, God still somewhat preserved the human
will for His purpose. When we believe in the Lord Jesus, this is
a strong determination on our part by the exercise of our will.
Martin Luther is an example of a person whose will was very
strong, so he had great faith. To have strong faith always
depends upon a very strong will.

A. Two Trees, Indicating Two Wills, Two Sources, and Two Possibilities for Man to Choose

God putting man before two trees indicates that man had a
free will. The two trees show that in this universe there are two
wills, two sources, and two possibilities for man to choose. God
put man before the two trees in a neutral position. This indicates that man surely by that time had a strong free will; otherwise, God would not have put him in front of two choices.

B. Being Charged to Eat the Right Tree, Indicating That God Created for Man a Free Will and That God Wanted Man to Exercise His Free Will to Choose Him

After God put man in front of two choices, God warned man
not to choose the wrong tree and charged him to eat the right
tree (Gen. 2:16-17). This indicates that God created for man a
free will and that God wanted man to exercise his free will to
choose Him.

V. GOD'S PROHIBITING MAN FROM EATING
THE TREE OF KNOWLEDGE INDICATING THAT GOD
WANTED MAN TO RECEIVE HIM AS LIFE
BY ENJOYING HIM

God's prohibiting man from eating the tree of knowledge indicates that God wanted man to receive Him as life by enjoying Him (John 1:11-12; Col. 2:6). To eat is a matter of enjoyment. God wanted man to receive Him in the way of joy, in the way of enjoyment, not in any other way.

VI. MAN NEEDING TO BE GOD'S VESSEL
TO CONTAIN HIM

Man has to be the vessel of God to contain Him. This is the concluding emphasis of this lesson. To emphasize this we should use Ephesians 3:17a—"That Christ may make His home in your hearts." We have to tell the saints that a home is a big vessel. All the dwellers are contained in their dwelling places. The house contains us. Thus, we have to be God's vessels to contain God.

In the book of Ephesians, Paul strongly charges us to be the home of Christ. He desired to see that Christ might make His home in our hearts so that we might be His real vessels. The teachings in Christianity miss this. They stress many other ethical things but not the point that we have to let the Lord make His home in our hearts so that we may be His vessels to contain Him. The focus of this lesson should be man being God's container.

GOD'S INTENTION IN MAN

Scripture Reading: Gen. 2:8-9, 16-17; Rev. 2:7; 22:14; John 6:35a, 57b

OUTLINE

I. Two choices remaining in front of man:
   A. The tree of life:
      1. Signifying God as life to man.
      2. Issuing in a dependent life.
   B. The tree of knowledge:
      1. Signifying Satan as evil to man.
      2. Issuing in an independent life.
II. God wanting man to receive Him as life by the way of eating:
   A. Eating being the unique way to receive nourishment organically.
   B. God being man's real food.
   C. To receive God by eating being to have God assimilated into man's being metabolically.
III. God forbidding man to eat the tree of knowledge:
   A. God's first commandment to man.
   B. Eating—to receive something in—being critical to man:
      1. After man was created, God not asking man to do anything.
      2. God only charging man not to eat wrongly.
   C. To eat the tree of knowledge being to receive Satan as an evil life into man's being.
   D. God's forbidding commandment being a warning to man:

1. Indicating God's greatness in dealing with man.
2. Indicating God's love to man.
3. Indicating God's desire that man would eat the tree of life to receive God into him as his life.

In this lesson we want to see God's intention in man.

I. TWO CHOICES REMAINING IN FRONT OF MAN

In Genesis 2 we see two choices remaining in front of man.

A. The Tree of Life

One of the two choices before man was the tree of life (vv. 8-9).

1. *Signifying God as Life to Man*

The tree of life signifies God as life to man.

2. *Issuing in a Dependent Life*

The tree of life issues in a dependent life. We need to develop this point so that the saints understand what we mean. The tree of life first signifies God as life to man. If man would take the tree of life, that would issue in a dependent life in man. Very few Christians realize that life always produces dependence. All the matters related to life are matters of dependence. You cannot graduate from any matter of life. Eating is a dependent matter. You cannot say that you have eaten the best food and that you have eaten more than enough, so you do not need to eat anymore. The matters of drinking and breathing, of course, are also dependent matters from which we do not graduate.

This shows that to take God as our life issues in a dependent life. Knowledge, on the other hand, issues in independence. If a person goes to college and gets a degree, he does not need that college any longer. When a person knows what his professor knows, he does not need to depend on his professor anymore. But if you were to take your professor as your life, you could never be independent from him. If you took him for your knowledge, you could be independent. But if you took him as your life, you could not be independent. You would have to be dependent upon him all the time.

God is not knowledge to us. God is life to us. We take Him as our life, and this divine life right away issues in a kind of dependence within us. We have to depend upon Him all the time. He is the vine, and we are the branches. The branches have to abide in the vine (John 15:5). Apart from the vine, the branches become dead. This vine tree's life issues in a kind of dependent life in all the branches. All the branches depend upon the vine's life.

The dependent life is also seen in Abraham's following the Lord. Hebrews 11:8 says, "By faith Abraham, being called, obeyed to go out unto a place which he was to receive as an inheritance; and he went out, not knowing where he was going." The Lord did not let Abraham know where he was going. He did not give Abraham a road map. Once the driver gets a road map from a person, he no longer needs that person. Because he has the map, he does not need to depend on the person who gave it to him. But if a person would give you himself, his presence, instead of a road map, you could never be independent from him. You would have to take him as your map, being dependent upon him all the time. That was the real case with Abraham. Abraham exercised his faith to trust in God for His instant leading, taking God's presence as the map for his traveling. Thus, Abraham became dependent upon God.

The God of glory appeared to Abraham (Acts 7:2), and that appearing issued in Abraham living a dependent life. Thus, taking the tree of life into us makes us dependent upon that life, the life of the tree of life, all the time. This is like the branches of the vine depending upon the vine, the life of the vine, all the time.

We have to stress again and again that the tree of life signifies God as life to man and that once man takes the tree of life, takes God as life, right away this divine life issues in a dependent life in man. Before taking this tree of life, the very God as life, man is independent. But after man takes the tree of life, God as life, it becomes absolutely impossible for man to be independent. Right away the divine life of God causes man to depend upon God all the time.

If we in the churches minister knowledge to people, they may learn the things we teach and then go their way. But if we minister life to people, they can never be independent. Life is not an independent matter but a dependent matter. Some people may come to the church, learn something, and then want to go away to do something, using what they have learned. They may take the knowledge they have acquired and be independent, but there will be no life in what they do. We need to be those who depend upon the tree of life, that is, God Himself as life to us.

B. The Tree of Knowledge

The other choice before man was the tree of knowledge.

1. Signifying Satan as Evil to Man

The tree of knowledge signifies Satan as evil to man. This evil is actually an evil life.

2. Issuing in an Independent Life

The tree of knowledge issues in a kind of independent life in you. The more knowledge you give people, the more independent they can become. Knowledge causes people to be independent. When you take in the tree of knowledge, you will feel that you do not need to depend upon God. Instead, you will depend upon your knowledge. But if you take in the tree of life, this causes you to depend upon God. Life is a matter of dependence, but knowledge is a matter of independence.

These critical points are pointed out by Brother Watchman Nee in a booklet entitled *Two Principles of Living.* These two principles are actually two lives. One is the dependent life and the other is the independent life. One is the principle of dependence and the other is the principle of independence. The tree of life issues in a principle of dependence, and the tree of knowledge issues in a principle of independence. Due to the fact that man took the tree of knowledge, man became altogether independent from God. But whoever repents to God and receives Him as life becomes dependent on God.

Before we were saved, we were altogether independent of God. But when we repented to God and believed in God, we became dependent. Whenever we have been independent, that was the time we lived by knowledge. Whenever we lived by our spirit, by life, we were altogether dependent upon God. Thus, these are two kinds of principles issuing from two kinds of lives. The divine life makes us dependent, and the satanic life makes us independent. To be independent means to be rebellious. To rebel means to be independent from God.

II. GOD WANTING MAN TO RECEIVE HIM AS LIFE
BY THE WAY OF EATING

God wanted man to receive Him as life by the way of eating.

A. Eating Being the Unique Way
to Receive Nourishment Organically

Eating is the unique way to receive nourishment organically. To receive anything organic, there is no other way except by eating. What you eat becomes your organic nourishment. We need to develop this point.

B. God Being Man's Real Food

Eating is the unique way, and God is the unique food to man. Here we have to tell people that all the physical food we eat is a shadow. God is the reality of our food. You can use Colossians 2:16-17 to show this.

C. To Receive God by Eating Being to Have God
Assimilated into Man's Being Metabolically

I like to use these two words—*organically* and *metabolically*. To receive God by eating Him is to have God assimilated into our being metabolically. When we receive God into us, His new element replaces what we are, and our old element is discharged. This is a kind of metabolism. Our physical, organic eating and metabolic digesting and assimilating are an illustration of the eating, digesting, and assimilating of Jesus as our spiritual food. This is not just our concept. This is the deep concept in the whole Bible.

When the Lord Jesus came, He said, "I am the bread of life" (John 6:35a), and "He who eats Me, he also shall live because of Me" (v. 57b). The tree of life is seen in Genesis 2 at the beginning of the Bible and in Revelation 2 and 22 at the end of the Bible. This tells us that the whole concept in the Bible is that man has to eat God, to take God in organically, and to assimilate God metabolically so that God may become his "fibers," his "tissue," his very being. The food that we eat eventually becomes our being. We become what we eat. We are a composition of the food that we have assimilated. God today is our food in the same principle.

In Revelation 2:7 the Lord Jesus promised the church in Ephesus that to the one who overcomes, He would give to eat of the tree of life. The last promise in the entire Bible is a promise of the enjoyment of the tree of life, which is Christ with all the riches of life (22:14).

III. GOD FORBIDDING MAN
TO EAT THE TREE OF KNOWLEDGE

God did not say anything to Adam regarding the tree of life, but God did say something regarding the tree of knowledge. God forbade man to eat the tree of knowledge (Gen. 2:17).

A. God's First Commandment to Man

God's first commandment to man was related to his eating. He charged man not to eat of the tree of the knowledge of good and evil.

B. Eating—to Receive Something In—
Being Critical to Man

Eating is critical to us because eating is to receive something into us. If you eat the right food, you will receive the nourishment. If you eat something poisonous, you will die. Parents hide all the poisonous things from their children and keep them out of their reach. Even the chemical and drug factories put a warning label on certain things to show that they are poisonous, or they may put their drugs in special containers that cannot be opened by children. What man takes into him is critical. It is a matter of life or death. Eating is critical to man.

1. After Man Was Created,
God Not Asking Man to Do Anything

After man was created, God did not ask man to do anything. God was concerned only about what His created man would eat.

2. God Only Charging Man Not to Eat Wrongly

God only charged man not to eat wrongly. How man would turn out and what man's destiny would be was altogether dependent upon what he would eat.

C. To Eat the Tree of Knowledge
Being to Receive Satan as an Evil Life
into Man's Being

When man ate the tree of knowledge, he received Satan as an evil life into his being. All these points regarding God's intention in man are altogether not according to man's natural concept. This is why we need to stress these points, expound them, and make them so clear and impressive to all the saints.

D. God's Forbidding Commandment
Being a Warning to Man

1. Indicating God's Greatness
in Dealing with Man

God's forbidding commandment was a warning to man, indicating that God was great in His dealing with man. Only a small man forces people to accept his opinion. No one who is great or honorable will coerce people.

2. Indicating God's Love to Man

God's forbidding commandment to man also indicates God's love to man. Because God loved man, He warned man not to eat the wrong thing.

3. Indicating God's Desire That Man
Would Eat the Tree of Life
to Receive God into Him as His Life

God's warning to man concerning not eating the tree of knowledge indicates three things: God's greatness, God's love, and God's desire. God's desire was that man would eat the tree of life to receive God into him as his life.

God did not force man to take what He wanted man to take, but He left this decision up to man. His warning man indicates that, on the one hand, He was great and, on the other hand, He was loving. He did not force man to do what He desired. This shows that He was great. Yet He warned man not to take the wrong thing, and this implies that God had love. He put man mainly in front of two trees, and He warned man not to take the tree of knowledge. This surely implies that God wanted man to take the tree of life. Thus, God's warning indicates His desire. God wanted man to take the tree of life, that is, God Himself, into man as man's life.

This lesson is very crucial. It is a kind of revolutionizing concept to the human mentality. We must have this lesson as a preparation for the saints to go on in life.

Question: What is the best way to show that the tree of the knowledge of good and evil represents Satan's life?

Answer: The Bible shows us that in this whole universe there are only two sources. Satan came in to seduce man to partake of the tree of knowledge. This means that Satan captured man by getting man to take him in. This is a big thing in the Bible. The tree of life and the tree of knowledge actually are the two controlling lines through the sixty-six books of the Bible.

In the families, in the nations, and even in the churches, God is here as the tree of life, and Satan is here as the tree of knowledge. Which way would you take, and whom would you contact? If you contact God, you get life and you depend upon God. If you take the tree of knowledge, you get Satan. If you get Satan, you become independent from God. To become independent means to rebel. The more you take the tree of knowledge, the more you rebel against God and become independent from God. When you take the tree of knowledge, you become one with Satan, who was and still is a rebel. If you take the tree of life, you are one with God and become dependent upon God.

These two principles are with us today, but most people always take the tree of knowledge. It is very rare to see persons who would take the tree of life. Even in our daily life, we have to admit that we take the tree of knowledge. When a husband argues with his wife, he is taking the tree of knowledge. The more we argue about who is wrong and who is right, the more of the tree of knowledge we eat. As a result, we become deadened and independent from God. Then we have to repent and confess. We have to get the cleansing of the precious blood, and the blood brings us back into contact with God. When we contact God again, we become dependent on God. The next time we are tempted to argue, we should say, "Lord, if You do not debate, I will not debate. If You do not argue, I will not argue.

I am one with You." We all need to live a dependent life of the tree of life and turn away from the tree of the knowledge of good and evil.

LESSON FOUR

SATAN'S PLOT TO SPOIL MAN

Scripture Reading: Gen. 3:1-7; Rom. 7:17-18a, 21, 23; Eph. 2:1, 12; 4:18

OUTLINE

   I. Being God's adversary—Matt. 13:28a.
  II. Hiding himself in the subtle serpent—Gen. 3:1a; 2 Cor. 11:3; Rev. 12:9a.
 III. Preventing God by contacting man earlier.
 IV. Approaching the woman by touching her mind—Gen. 3:1b.
  V. Causing the human mind to doubt God's word—v. 4.
 VI. Stirring up the human emotion to dislike God—v. 5.
VII. Seducing the human will to choose the tree of knowledge—v. 6a.
VIII. Contaminating the entire human soul.
 IX. Entering into the human body to be the evil in man's flesh—Rom. 7:17-18a, 21, 23.
  X. Capturing man through the woman—Gen. 3:6b; 1 Tim. 2:14.
 XI. Becoming one with man and alienating man from God by deadening man's spirit—Eph. 2:1, 12; 4:18.
XII. Usurping man to frustrate God from fulfilling His purpose.

In this lesson on life, we want to see Satan's plot to spoil man.

I. BEING GOD'S ADVERSARY

Satan is God's adversary. Matthew 13:28a is nearly the only verse in the New Testament that tells us that Satan is God's enemy. In Matthew 13:28 the word *enemy* is used, but we have to realize that Satan is not only God's enemy but also God's adversary. This is because he is within the circle where God is (Job 1:6). The name Satan, from Hebrew, means "adversary." He was and still is not only an enemy from outside but also an adversary from inside. We have to point out that in the universe God has an enemy and even an adversary within His kingdom.

II. HIDING HIMSELF IN THE SUBTLE SERPENT

Genesis 3:1 shows that Satan hid himself in the subtle serpent. For this point we can also use 2 Corinthians 11:3 and Revelation 12:9. Satan is always hiding himself in some thing, in some matter, or even in some person. In Matthew 16 Satan was hiding himself in Peter, so the Lord Jesus even called Peter "Satan" (v. 23). When Satan first came to man, he was hiding himself in a serpent. Because Satan was hiding himself in the serpent, eventually his name is called the ancient serpent in Revelation 12:9.

III. PREVENTING GOD BY CONTACTING MAN EARLIER

In this point we have to make it clear that God's intention was to enter into man to be man's life. But in the Bible we can see that when Satan realizes that God intends to do something, he will do it earlier, to prevent God from carrying out His intention. Thus, before God came to enter into man, Satan came. Because God is great, He would not force man to choose Him and receive Him. Satan acted first to enter into man earlier than God in an attempt to prevent God from carrying out His desire with man.

It seems that God always comes later than we expect Him. John 11 tells us that when the Lord heard that Lazarus was sick, He remained in the place where He was for two days (v. 6).

During this time Lazarus died, and then the Lord went to raise him from the dead. Martha and Mary both told the Lord, "If You had been here, my brother would not have died" (vv. 21, 32). In the Bible there are many instances to show us that God would not do things that fast. But do not stress this point in your sharing. If you stress this point, you may distract the saints. You must stress the point that Satan came to contact man earlier than God did.

IV. APPROACHING THE WOMAN
BY TOUCHING HER MIND

The subtle adversary of God approached the female, the weaker vessel, by touching her mind. In Genesis 3:1b he asked the woman, "Did God really say, You shall not eat of any tree of the garden?" This was a question put into Eve's mind, and this question stirred up her doubting mind. This is a strong point that we have to stress. Satan would always approach people by touching their doubting mind. Here Satan questioned something concerning God, and this questioning, no doubt, aroused the mind of Eve. Satan did this to keep Eve from using her spirit. When God comes to us, He always touches our spirit. When Satan comes to us, he always comes to our mind. Our spirit is the "room" that God comes to touch, and our mind is the "room" that Satan comes to touch. Satan will always come to touch the human mind.

V. CAUSING THE HUMAN MIND
TO DOUBT GOD'S WORD

After Satan came to touch the female mind, he caused the human mind to doubt God's word (v. 4). In verse 1 of Genesis 3, he stirred up Eve's mind; then in verses 2 and 3 Eve began to talk to him. This meant that Eve had fallen into the snare already. Eve should not have talked with the serpent or answered him. She should have stood on God's word and run away from this tempter. Instead of running away, she responded by saying, "Of the fruit of the trees of the garden we may eat; but of the fruit of the tree which is in the middle of the garden, God has said, You shall not eat of it, nor shall you touch it, lest you die" (vv. 2-3). This little talk meant that Eve had fallen into the snare already. Her answer opened the door for the serpent to say to the woman, "You shall not surely die!" (v. 4). This is a further step Satan took to deal with the female mind. Satan not only came to touch her mind, but eventually Satan caused the human mind to doubt God's word. This means that the poison of the serpent got into her mind, because the word of Satan got into her. When the word gets in, the person gets in. Thus, the human mind was poisoned, contaminated.

VI. STIRRING UP THE HUMAN EMOTION TO DISLIKE GOD

Satan also stirred up the human emotion to dislike God. This is proved by verse 5, where Satan said to Eve, "God knows that in the day you eat of it your eyes will be opened, and you will become like God, knowing good and evil." This word was a word of evil, stirring up Eve's emotion to dislike God. Eve probably felt that God had kept some good thing from her. This is the subtlety of the enemy to poison the human emotion.

VII. SEDUCING THE HUMAN WILL TO CHOOSE THE TREE OF KNOWLEDGE

Satan seduced the human will to choose the tree of knowledge. After Satan's word in verse 5, verse 6 says, "When the woman saw that the tree was good for food and that it was a delight to the eyes and that the tree was to be desired to make oneself wise, she took of its fruit and ate." This is the seducing of the human will to make a decision to partake of the tree of the knowledge of good and evil.

VIII. CONTAMINATING THE ENTIRE HUMAN SOUL

At this point, Satan had contaminated the entire human soul: the mind, the emotion, and the will. The mind was poisoned, the emotion was poisoned, and the will was poisoned; thus, the entire soul was contaminated.

IX. ENTERING INTO THE HUMAN BODY TO BE THE EVIL IN MAN'S FLESH

When Eve and Adam took the fruit of the tree of knowledge, Satan entered into the human body to be the evil in man's flesh. Here we must use Romans 7:17-18a. Paul says, "Now then it is no longer I that work it out but sin that dwells in me. For I know that in me, that is, in my flesh, nothing good dwells." Paul says that in his flesh there was no good thing. Then Romans 7:21 says, "I find then the law with me who wills to do the good, that is, the evil is present with me." "The evil" must be the evil life, nature, and character of Satan himself, who is the indwelling sin in us. When sin is dormant within us, it is merely sin, but when it is aroused in us by our willing to do the good, it becomes "the evil." Verse 23 says, "I see a different law in my members, warring against the law of my mind and making me a captive to the law of sin which is in my members." Sin and evil are in man's members, in the flesh. This shows us that when man partook of the tree of knowledge, his whole being was taken over by Satan.

X. CAPTURING MAN THROUGH THE WOMAN

Satan captured man through the woman (Gen. 3:6b). He first secured the weaker vessel, woman, and then he used the woman to capture man. First Timothy 2:14 says, "Adam was not deceived; but the woman, having been quite deceived, has fallen into transgression." It was not man who was deceived but the woman. History tells us that Satan frequently uses the female to gain the male and corrupt him.

XI. BECOMING ONE WITH MAN
AND ALIENATING MAN FROM GOD
BY DEADENING MAN'S SPIRIT

Satan became one with man and alienated man from God by deadening man's spirit. Here we have to use Ephesians 2:1 and 12 and 4:18. In these verses we can see that man was deadened in the spirit. By this, man was alienated, cut off, from God and even cut off from the life of God. We can see that man had fallen to the uttermost. The mind was poisoned, the emotion was poisoned, the will was poisoned, and the body was poisoned. Also man's spirit was deadened. The whole being of man thus became contaminated, deadened, and alienated from God.

XII. USURPING MAN TO FRUSTRATE GOD FROM FULFILLING HIS PURPOSE

Satan usurped man to frustrate God from fulfilling His purpose. Today mankind is in the hand of Satan, and Satan uses the whole human race to do his will, to frustrate God from fulfilling God's purpose. Man was made by God to fulfill God's purpose. But man fell into the usurping hand of Satan, so man is being used by Satan to fulfill Satan's purpose. This is the plot of Satan to spoil man.

We have to stress that Satan spoiled man by contaminating man's soul and deadening his spirit. We also have to point out that man's body was ruined to become the flesh. In the flesh, man's ruined body, there is sin, and when this sin acts, it is "the evil" (Rom. 7:21). Sin and evil are the same thing. The term *sin* mostly denotes the nature, whereas the term *the evil* mostly denotes the activities. Actually, both sin and the evil are Satan himself. Satan himself in our flesh is sin. When sin acts, it is the evil. We can see that the whole human being became utterly fallen by eating the tree of knowledge. The soul was contaminated, the spirit was deadened, and the body was ruined.

We have to pray so that we can have the best utterance to present these things to the new ones and to the young ones. I feel that this is quite crucial for the coming lessons on life.

THE REAL SIGNIFICANCE OF MAN'S FALL

Scripture Reading: Gen. 3:1-8; Rom. 5:12, 14-16; 7:14b, 17-18, 20-21; Eph. 2:1, 5a; 4:18; 1 Cor. 15:22a

OUTLINE

I. Not only:
  A. Transgressing against God's commandment—Rom. 5:14b.
  B. Falling under God's condemnation—v. 16b.
  C. Estranging man from God—Gen. 3:8; Eph. 4:18.
  D. Spoiling man from fulfilling God's purpose:
    1. Expressing God in His image.
    2. Representing God with His dominion.

II. But also:
  A. Receiving Satan's evil thought, feeling, and will into the inward parts of man's soul—Gen. 3:1, 4-5.
  B. Taking the tree of knowledge into the members of man's body—3:6:
    1. Man's body being transmuted into flesh—Rom. 7:18a.
    2. Satan becoming sin within man—vv. 14b, 17, 20.
    3. Sin acting as evil in man—v. 21.
  C. Deadening man's spirit—Eph. 2:1, 5a.
  D. Letting sin enter into man—Rom. 5:12a.
  E. Making man the victim of death—vv. 12b, 14a; 1 Cor. 15:22a.

Focus: Through man's fall Satan's personality became one with man's soul, and he was taken into man's body to be sin working as evil in man's fleshly members.

In the previous lesson we saw Satan's plot to spoil man. In this lesson we want to see the real significance of man's fall. Among most Christians the understanding of man's fall is altogether inadequate. For this lesson we need to read the verses in the Scripture Reading attentively, slowly, and carefully so that we can be impressed with these portions of the Word.

I. NOT ONLY:

A. Transgressing against God's Commandment

Romans 5:14 refers to "Adam's transgression." Adam transgressed against God's commandment. Man's fall was a transgression against God's first commandment. Adam forsook the tree of life, which denotes God as life, to pursue the tree of knowledge, which signifies Satan as the source of death (Gen. 2:8-9, 17; 3:1-7).

B. Falling under God's Condemnation

Adam's one offense caused man to fall under God's condemnation. Romans 5:16 speaks of Adam's "one offense unto condemnation." Man transgressed against God's commandment and fell under God's condemnation.

C. Estranging Man from God

Man's fall estranged man from God. Genesis 3:8 says that man hid himself from God's presence. Right after man's fall, man hid himself. This means that man was estranged from God. Ephesians 4:18 tells us that man in his fallen state is "alienated from the life of God."

D. Spoiling Man from Fulfilling God's Purpose

Man's fall spoiled man from fulfilling God's purpose, which is to express God in His image and represent God with His dominion (Gen. 1:26).

II. BUT ALSO:

A. Receiving Satan's Evil Thought, Feeling, and Will into the Inward Parts of Man's Soul

Through his fall, man received Satan's evil thought, feeling, and will into the inward parts of his soul. For this point we need to read Genesis 3:1, 4, and 5 to show that Satan's thought was injected into man's mind, his feeling was injected into man's emotion, and his will was injected into man's will. This means that man's soul was stolen by his fall; it was taken over by Satan.

B. Taking the Tree of Knowledge into the Members of Man's Body

Genesis 3:6 says that Eve ate the fruit of the tree of knowledge, gave it to Adam, her husband, and he also ate of it. What people eat gets into their physical body. By eating the tree of knowledge, man took the tree of knowledge into the members of his body.

1. Man's Body Being Transmuted into Flesh

God created man with a pure body, but something of Satan was received into man's body, and man's body changed in nature. It was transmuted into the flesh. In other words, it was corrupted. Man's body, by being corrupted in man's fall, became flesh, full of lust. In Romans 7:18a Paul says, "I know that in me, that is, in my flesh, nothing good dwells." The flesh is the corrupted body.

2. Satan Becoming Sin within Man

Through man's eating the tree of knowledge, Satan entered into man and became the very sin within man. To see this point we need to read Romans 7:14b, 17, and 20. In verse 20 Paul says, "If what I do not will, this I do, it is no longer I that work it out but sin that dwells in me." Romans 7, especially in verses 8, 11, 17, and 20, indicates that sin is a person, the embodiment of Satan, and is living and acting within us. Sin is a personification of Satan. Actually speaking, the sin within us is Satan. At least we can say that the sinful nature within man is the nature of Satan. The sin within man refers to his inward sinful nature. This inward sin is just Satan himself indwelling our corrupted body, that is, our flesh.

3. Sin Acting as Evil in Man

In Romans 7:21 Paul says, "I find then the law with me who wills to do the good, that is, the evil is present with me." When Satan entered into man, Satan became sin within man. When this sin acts in man, this sin becomes "the evil." The evil is the action of sin. When sin acts in us, it becomes the evil.

The real significance of man's fall is that man received Satan's thought, feeling, and will, Satan's being, Satan's personality, into the inward parts of his soul. Thus, man's soul became one with Satan's person through man's fall. Also, Satan as sin got into man's body, making man's body the flesh. Satan indwells this flesh as sin, as fallen man's sinful nature. When this sin acts, it is the very evil that moves and acts within man. Through the fall, man's being, man's personality, man's soul, has been filled with Satan's being, with Satan's personality. Satan dwells in man's body as sin, which acts as the evil. Thus, through man's fall, man became one with Satan. This is the reason that the children of men eventually are called in the Bible the children of the devil (1 John 3:10). Fallen man became one with Satan in his personality and in his nature. Man and Satan are one, so the children of men actually are the children of the devil. This is the focus and the real significance of man's fall. We need to point out that man's fall was a receiving of Satan's being into man's being and a taking of Satan himself into man's body, corrupting man's body and transmuting it into the flesh.

C. Deadening Man's Spirit

Man's fall also resulted in the deadening of his spirit (Eph. 2:1, 5a). Ephesians 2:1 says that in our fallen state we were dead in our offenses and sins. This means that our spirit was deadened. To be deadened means that the function of our spirit was damaged. The deadness of our spirit pervaded our entire being and caused us to lose the function that enabled us to contact God. Thus, through the fall, man's soul became one with Satan's person, man's body became Satan's dwelling place, and man's spirit was deadened.

D. Letting Sin Enter into Man

Through man's fall, man let sin enter into him. Romans 5:12a says that through one man sin entered into the world. Actually, *the world* here means mankind. When sin entered into man, that really meant that Satan entered into man.

E. Making Man the Victim of Death

The real significance of man's fall is that Satan was taken into man, sin entered into man, and man became a victim of death (vv. 12b, 14a; 1 Cor. 15:22a). Romans 5:12b points out that through sin entering into the world, death passed on to all men. Death is the ultimate result of man's fall. Romans 5:14a says that from Adam to Moses, death reigned. Death even became a king. First Corinthians 15:22a says that in Adam all die. Thus, all mankind is a victim of death through man's fall.

In this lesson we have to stress how man became one with Satan in his three parts. Every part of man was ruined, corrupted, and deadened, making man a hopeless case. Sin entered into man, moving, damaging, and killing man, and man is now altogether under the tyranny of death. Man is a victim of death. It is not just man transgressing against God, not just man falling under God's condemnation, but man receiving Satan into himself. Satan's being entered into man's being, and Satan himself as sin entered into man's body, making man's body the flesh. Through all this, man's spirit was also deadened.

We must make all these points so clear and so impressive to the saints. Then we can go on to help the saints to see the need of life. There is not just the need of an objective salvation but the need of a subjective life. Lesson 4 and this lesson are crucial so that we can have the proper experience of life.

We must do a good work to make all the saints clear about how Satan spoiled man and how man fell. It is not just a matter of man transgressing against God and falling under God's condemnation but a matter of man taking in something. We may use the illustration of a mother warning her child not to take in something poisonous. This is the mother's commandment. If the mother leaves home and the child takes in that poison, this is not merely a transgression against the mother's commandment. It is a receiving of the poison into the child's being. This is an illustration of what happened when man fell. When God comes in to save us, He does not just take care of our transgression and of our being under His condemnation. He also works to take away the poison and to rescue us from death.

LESSON SIX

THE SALVATION OF LIFE

Scripture Reading: John 1:4a; 10:10b; 1 Cor. 15:45b; Eph. 2:5;
Rom. 5:10b; 8:2

OUTLINE

    I. Satan having the might of death—Heb. 2:14b.

    II. Death being the ultimate issue of Satan's plot concerning man—Gen. 2:17b.

    III. Death coming in through sin—Rom. 5:12b.

    IV. Man being dead in sins—Eph. 2:1.

    V. Man's body being of death—Rom. 7:24b; 8:10b.

    VI. Man's mind set on the flesh being death—v. 6a.

    VII. The Son of God coming as life—John 1:4a; 10:10b; 11:25a; 1 John 5:12a.

    VIII. The Son of God having nullified death and destroyed Satan who has the might of death—2 Tim. 1:10b; Heb. 2:14b.

    IX. The Son of God having released life and imparted it into God's chosen people—John 12:24; 19:34b; 2 Tim. 1:10b; 1 Pet. 1:3b.

    X. Christ having become the life-giving Spirit—1 Cor. 15:45b; 2 Cor. 3:6b, 17a.

    XI. God having saved us by enlivening us—Eph. 2:5.

    XII. God now saving us in the life of His Son—Rom. 5:10b.

    XIII. Christ now being our life and living in us—Col. 3:4a; Gal. 2:20b.

    XIV. The law of the Spirit of life freeing us from the law of sin and of death—Rom. 8:2.

XV. Eating the bread of life, drinking the water of life, and living by the Son of God as our life—John 6:35, 57b; 7:37-39; Rev. 21:6b; 22:17b.

Focus: God's salvation is not only by the death of Christ but also by His life to save us from both sin and death.

In the past few lessons, we have laid a foundation mostly on the negative side. Now we want to go on to see the positive side. In this lesson there are fifteen main points.

I. SATAN HAVING THE MIGHT OF DEATH

First, we have to point out that Satan has the might of death. Hebrews 2:14b says that the devil has the might of death.

II. DEATH BEING THE ULTIMATE ISSUE OF SATAN'S PLOT CONCERNING MAN

Death is the ultimate issue of Satan's plot concerning man. Satan's plot is to bring man into death. In Genesis 2:17 God warned man that partaking of the tree of knowledge would cause him to die. Actually, this was a warning that man should not have any contact with Satan. If man would have some contact with Satan, the result, the issue, would be death.

III. DEATH COMING IN THROUGH SIN

Romans 5:12b tells us that death came in through sin. Satan seduced man to commit sin. Through sin, death came into man. Thus, sin was not the actual issue of man's fall, but death.

IV. MAN BEING DEAD IN SINS

Ephesians 2:1 says that man is dead in sins. Satan brought man into death through sin, and today Satan keeps all men in sins so that death may continue to work in man and on man. All men are dead because all are under sin.

V. MAN'S BODY BEING OF DEATH

Man's body is now a body of death. In Romans 7:24 the body is called "the body of this death." This is the killing death that utterly weakens and disables the corrupted body so that it cannot keep God's commandments. Man's body is of such a present killing death, so Paul says that "the body is dead" (8:10). Romans 7 shows that despite man's mind wanting to do good, man's body, being of the killing death, will not allow man's mind to work out what the mind wants. In Romans 7 the warfare is between man's mind and man's body. Because man's body is of such a present killing death, it prevails against man's mind.

VI. MAN'S MIND SET ON THE FLESH BEING DEATH

Romans 8:6a says, "The mind set on the flesh is death." Man's mind wants to do good, but if man's mind is set on the flesh, on the corrupted body, man's mind also becomes death. Thus, we see from the points above that man is dead in sins, that man's body is of the killing death, and that man's mind can also become death if it is set upon the corrupted body. Satan has the might of death, and Satan has brought man into death. Now man is dead, man's body is of death, and man's mind set on the flesh is death.

VII. THE SON OF GOD COMING AS LIFE

In order to save man from both sin and death, the Son of God came as life (John 1:4a; 10:10b; 11:25a; 1 John 5:12a). Generally speaking, Christianity mostly stresses that the Son of God came to accomplish redemption for us. They do not stress that the Son of God came as life to save us by His life. We need to stress the verse references above from John's writings to show that the Son of God came as life that we may have life.

VIII. THE SON OF GOD HAVING NULLIFIED DEATH AND DESTROYED SATAN WHO HAS THE MIGHT OF DEATH

The Son of God has nullified death and destroyed Satan who has the might of death. Second Timothy 1:10 says that the Son of God has nullified death, and Hebrews 2:14b says that the Son of God has destroyed the devil who has the might of death. These two verses give us a clear vision that after the Son of God came, He nullified death and also destroyed the source of death, that is, the devil, who has the might of death.

IX. THE SON OF GOD HAVING RELEASED LIFE AND IMPARTED IT INTO GOD'S CHOSEN PEOPLE

The Bible reveals that the Son of God released life and imparted it into God's chosen people. John 12:24 speaks of Christ as the one grain of wheat who died to release His life to produce us as the many grains. In John 19:34b not only blood but also water came out of the pierced side of Christ. This means that life was released through His death. Second Timothy 1:10 says that the Son of God brought life to light; this means that He released life and manifested life. First Peter 1:3b says that through the resurrection of Christ, God has regenerated us. This means that after Christ released the life within Him through His death, He imparted His life in resurrection to God's chosen people.

X. CHRIST HAVING BECOME THE LIFE-GIVING SPIRIT

Christ has become the life-giving Spirit (1 Cor. 15:45b). After Christ released His life through death and imparted this life to God's chosen people through His resurrection, He Himself became the life-giving Spirit. Therefore, 2 Corinthians 3 says that the Spirit gives life (v. 6b) and that now the Lord is the Spirit (v. 17). He came as life. Then on the cross He destroyed death and the source of death, and He released life to God's chosen people. Finally, in resurrection He became the life-giving Spirit so that He may impart Himself as life into us, enter into us, and live within us.

XI. GOD HAVING SAVED US BY ENLIVENING US

God has saved us by enlivening us. Ephesians 2:5 says that we have been saved by grace. Christianity has misused this verse. They use this verse for salvation by the death of Christ. Actually, Ephesians 2:5 refers not to the salvation by Christ's death but to the salvation by Christ's life. This is because Ephesians 2 tells us that we were saved by being made alive together with Christ and by being raised up from the dead (vv. 5-6). Thus, Ephesians 2 reveals a salvation not by Christ's death but by His life. God used the resurrection life to save us not from sin but from death. Romans 1 tells us that we are under sin and that we are sinners. But Ephesians 2 tells us that we are under death and that we are dead persons in sins. When we were dead in sins, God made us alive; He enlivened us by the resurrection life of Christ. Thus, it is the salvation of life, not the salvation by Christ's death.

XII. GOD NOW SAVING US IN THE LIFE OF HIS SON

God is now saving us in the life of His Son. Romans 5:10 says, "If we, being enemies, were reconciled to God through the death of His Son, much more we will be saved in His life, having been reconciled." Here it is not only the salvation of life but also the salvation of life in our daily life. Ephesians 2:5 says that we were saved at the time we believed by being made alive. Romans 5:10 says that after we have been saved by being made alive, God is still saving us by the life of Christ. This is our daily salvation. The salvation of life in Ephesians 2 is the saving at the time we believe, and in Romans 5 it is the saving in our daily life continually, day by day. This saving life is saving us all the time.

XIII. CHRIST NOW BEING OUR LIFE AND LIVING IN US

Christ is now our life, and He is living in us. Colossians 3:4a speaks of Christ our life, and Galatians 2:20 says that Christ lives in us. Christ is now our life and is now living in us to save us throughout the day.

XIV. THE LAW OF THE SPIRIT OF LIFE FREEING US FROM THE LAW OF SIN AND OF DEATH

Romans 8:2 says that the law of the Spirit of life frees us from the law of sin and of death. This law of the Spirit of life is the spontaneous function of Christ's resurrection life. The reality of this resurrection life is the Spirit, so the Spirit is called the Spirit of life. The spontaneous function of Christ's resurrection life is called the law of the Spirit of life. This law, this spontaneous function, frees us from the law of sin and of death. This is the salvation by and of life.

XV. EATING THE BREAD OF LIFE, DRINKING THE WATER OF LIFE, AND LIVING BY THE SON OF GOD AS OUR LIFE

We need to be those who eat the bread of life, drink the water of life, and live by the Son of God as our life (John 6:35, 57b; 7:37-39; Rev. 21:6b; 22:17b). In this last point we have to stress that what we need today in order to participate in this salvation of life is to eat the bread of life, to drink the water of life, and to live by Christ as our life. Then we are enjoying and experiencing the salvation of life.

We need to pay our attention to the focus of this lesson: God's salvation is not only by the death of Christ but also by His life to save us from both sin and death.

LESSON SEVEN

THE DEFINITION OF LIFE

Scripture Reading: Eph. 4:18; Rev. 22:1; John 14:6a; 1 John
1:2; 5:12a; Col. 3:4a; Rom. 8:2a; 2 Cor. 3:6b

OUTLINE

I. Life is not devotion:
  A. Devotion is our exercise of piety.
  B. Life is Christ living in us—Gal. 2:20a.
II. Life is not good behavior:
  A. Good behavior is our doing.
  B. Life is Christ lived out from us—Phil. 1:21a.
III. Life is not power:
  A. Power is for work—Acts 1:8.
  B. Life is for living—John 6:57b.
IV. Life is not gift:
  A. Gift is the ability for function—Rom. 12:6.
  B. Life is the divine being in our being—John 1:13b.
V. Life is not the growth in knowledge:
  A. The growth in knowledge is the increase of knowl-
     edge.
  B. Life is the increase of God—Col. 2:19b.
VI. Life is not our human life:
  A. Our human life (bios and psuche) is mortal—Luke
     8:43b; 21:4b; Matt. 16:25-26.
  B. Life (zoe) is eternal—1 John 1:2; Psa. 90:2b.
VII. Life is God's content and God's flowing out:
  A. God's content is God's being—Eph. 4:18a.
  B. God's flowing out is the impartation of Himself as
     life to us—Rev. 22:1.

VIII. Life is Christ—John 14:6a; Col. 3:4a; 1 John 5:12a:
   A. Christ is the embodiment of God who is life—Col. 2:9.
   B. Christ is the expression of God—John 1:18; Heb. 1:3a.
   IX. Life is the Holy Spirit:
   A. The Holy Spirit is the reality of Christ—John 14:16-17; 1 Cor. 15:45b.
   B. The Holy Spirit is the Spirit of life who gives life to us—Rom. 8:2a; 2 Cor. 3:6b.

Focus: Life is the Triune God dispensed into us and living in us.

We need to know what life is, so this lesson is on the definition of life. All the verses cited in the Scripture Reading above are very crucial. Ephesians 4:18 speaks of being alienated from the life of God. Revelation 22:1 says that out of the throne flows the river of water of life. In John 14:6a the Lord said that He is the life. First John 1:2 mentions the eternal life. First John 5:12a says that he who has the Son has the life. Colossians 3:4a refers to Christ our life. Romans 8:2a uses the phrase *the Spirit of life,* and 2 Corinthians 3:6b says that the Spirit gives life. These verses are crucial to our understanding of the definition of life.

I. LIFE IS NOT DEVOTION

The first point we need to see is that life is not devotion. Many Christians consider devotion to be the spiritual life, but devotion is our exercise of piety. It is an exercise on our side by our own effort. Paul says in Galatians 2:20a, "I am crucified with Christ; and it is no longer I who live, but it is Christ who lives in me." This shows that life is Christ living within us. We need to help the saints to realize that we should never consider devotion as life. One may be very devotional and yet not have much life. Some nuns and priests in the Catholic Church may be very devotional, but that is merely their kind of pious exercise. Life is not any kind of activity. Life is altogether Christ Himself. We must stress this to the uttermost, helping the saints to know that life is Christ Himself. Nothing can replace life.

II. LIFE IS NOT GOOD BEHAVIOR

Generally speaking, Christians consider that if a person's behavior is good, he has life. When I was in China, I observed that a number of the disciples of Confucius behaved better than the Christian missionaries. They were so gentle, patient, and humble. They were also very meek, having the virtue of giving in to others. But this is not life. This is merely good behavior. Confucius said that we need to develop the "bright virtue" within us, which is actually the development of our conscience. But we need to stress that life is not good behavior springing from our own effort to develop our conscience. Life is Christ.

Man was created good, but man was corrupted and damaged

by the fall. Still there is something good within man, which was created by God. The teachings of Confucius are to help develop man's good nature—the natural, good virtues created by God within man. These virtues have been damaged but are still left in man's nature. The good behavior developed by man is according to his doing, but life is Christ lived out from us. Life is not our doing. Paul says in Philippians 1:21a, "To me, to live is Christ." Thus, life is not good behavior; it is Christ lived out of us. First Christ lives within us, and then Christ lives Himself out of us. This is life.

We have to train the saints to discern the difference between good behavior and life. We may admire a certain brother because he is gentle, meek, humble, and patient. We may think that he is full of life, but this means that we do not have the proper discernment. This brother whom we admire may be expressing his natural virtues in his good behavior. Life, however, is Christ expressed from within us and lived out from within us.

III. LIFE IS NOT POWER

We also need to see that life is not power. The Spirit has two aspects: the aspect of life within us and the aspect of power upon us. When the New Testament talks about the Spirit's power, it uses the preposition *upon*. *Upon* means outside. When the New Testament speaks concerning the Spirit as life, it uses the preposition *in*. The Spirit is in us.

The New Testament says that the Spirit of reality will be with you and even in you, and the rivers of living water will flow out from within you. There is the aspect of drinking the Spirit and the aspect of being baptized in the Spirit. To baptize a person is to put him into the water, but to drink is to take in the water. First Corinthians 12:13 covers these two aspects. We all have been baptized in one Spirit into one Body. Then we all have been given to drink one Spirit. These are the two aspects concerning the Spirit. But in today's Christianity the life side is nearly neglected, and the power side is overemphasized wrongly. Therefore, we have to point out that life is not power.

Acts 1:8 shows that the Spirit of power coming upon the disciples enabled them to carry out the work of spreading the gospel from Jerusalem to the uttermost part of the earth. This verse shows us that power is for work, and John 6:57b shows that life is for living. In this verse the Lord said, "He who eats Me, he also shall live because of Me."

IV. LIFE IS NOT GIFT

Life is not gift. Gift is the ability for function (Rom. 12:6), but life is the Divine Being in our being. John 1:13b says that we believers are begotten of God. To be begotten of God is to have God's being in our being. Life is God Himself, the Divine Being, in our being.

V. LIFE IS NOT THE GROWTH IN KNOWLEDGE

The growth in knowledge is not life. The growth in knowledge is the increase of knowledge. You may accumulate a lot of biblical knowledge by reading books or by studying in a seminary and yet not know life at all. Life is the increase of God within us. Colossians 2:19b reveals that the church grows with the growth of God, with the increase of God as life.

VI. LIFE IS NOT OUR HUMAN LIFE

Our human life is not the life on which the Bible focuses. Our human life (bios and psuche) is mortal (Luke 8:43b; 21:4b; Matt. 16:25-26). Our human life is not life, because it dies and is destined to die. The real life is immortal. Whatever is mortal is not life. Both our physical life (bios) and our soulish life (psuche) are mortal, so the human life is not life. In Luke 8:43b and 21:4b the Greek word for *livelihood* and *living* is *bios*. *Bios* refers to the physical life. In Matthew 16:25-26 the Greek word for *soul-life* is *psuche*.

Life (zoe) is eternal. *Eternal* means "immortal." First John 1:2 says, "The life was manifested, and we have seen and testify and report to you the eternal life, which was with the Father and was manifested to us." Then Psalm 90:2b says, "Indeed from eternity to eternity, You are God." Strictly speaking, all lives that are mortal are not life. The real life is immortal and eternal, and this real life is God Himself because God is from eternity to eternity. God is eternal, so only God Himself is the real life.

VII. LIFE IS GOD'S CONTENT AND GOD'S FLOWING OUT

The six foregoing points tell us what is not life. Now we need to see what life is. Life is God's content and God's flowing out. God's content is God's being, so life is God's inner being (Eph. 4:18a). God's flowing out is the impartation of Himself as life to us. In Revelation 22:1 we see the river of water of life flowing out from the throne of God. This is God's flowing out. Life is God's content, His inner being, and life is God flowing out into us and being imparted into our being.

VIII. LIFE IS CHRIST

We need to impress the saints that life is Christ (John 14:6a; Col. 3:4a; 1 John 5:12a). Christ is the embodiment of God, who is life. Colossians 2:9 says that all the fullness of the Godhead dwells in Christ bodily. God as life is embodied in Christ, and Christ is the expression of God. John 1:18 says that no one has ever seen God, but the only begotten Son has declared Him. Then Hebrews 1:3 shows that Christ is the effulgence of God's glory. This means that Christ is the expression of God, who is life.

IX. LIFE IS THE HOLY SPIRIT

Finally, we need to point out that life is the Holy Spirit. The Holy Spirit is the reality of Christ (John 14:16-17; 1 Cor. 15:45b). The Son is the embodiment of the Father, and the Spirit is the reality of the Son. Romans 8:2a uses the term *the Spirit of life,* and 2 Corinthians 3:6b says that the Spirit gives life. Thus, the Holy Spirit today is the Spirit of life who gives life to us. We must stress that the Spirit in the New Testament has two aspects. On the one hand, He is the Spirit of power; on the other hand, He is the Spirit of life.

We need to pay attention to the focus of this lesson: life is the Triune God dispensed into us and living in us. The Father is the source, the Son is the course, and the Spirit is the flow. The Triune God is dispensed into us in His Divine Trinity and is now living within us.

Such a lesson on the definition of life is greatly needed among us. We may use the term *life* and yet not know what life is. We have to enter into a full understanding of what life is.

REGENERATION

Scripture Reading: John 3:3-8, 36; 1:12-13; 1 Pet. 1:3, 23;
James 1:18; 1 Cor. 4:15; 1 John 1:2; 2 Pet. 1:4

OUTLINE

  I. The definition of regeneration—John 1:13.
 II. The way:
    A. To realize our need of the life of God—3:3.
    B. To realize that our natural being needs to be buried
       in the water of baptism—v. 5.
    C. To be born of the Spirit of God in our spirit—
       vv. 5, 6b.
       1. By believing into the Son of God—v. 36a.
       2. Through the word of God in the gospel—1 Pet.
          1:23; James 1:18; 1 Cor. 4:15.
III. The issue:
    A. Resurrected with Christ—1 Pet. 1:3b; Eph. 2:5a.
    B. Having the eternal and uncreated life—1 John 1:2.
    C. Becoming a child of God—John 1:12.
    D. Partaking of the divine nature—2 Pet. 1:4.
    E. Born into the kingdom of God—John 3:5.

Focus: To be regenerated is to have the life of God so that we
      may be His children living in His kingdom according
      to the divine nature.

In the previous lessons, a foundation concerning life has been laid. Now we can get into the experiences of life, and the first experience of life is regeneration.

I. THE DEFINITION OF REGENERATION

First, we need to see the definition of regeneration. To be regenerated is to be born of God so that we may have the divine life, a life other than our human life. We have to impress all the saints with this clear definition of regeneration. This definition has not been made clear to most Christians. When I was young, I read a book on the real definition of regeneration, but the definition it presented was wrong. This book said that regeneration is the new beginning we have when we repent and all our sins are forgiven and considered as something in the past. Regeneration, however, is not merely a new beginning. This thought somewhat matches the teaching of Confucius, who said that whenever you repent, you can consider that everything is new from that day.

One day I read a book by Brother T. Austin-Sparks, which said that to be born again is to receive another life, the eternal and uncreated life of God, in addition to our human life. He gave a brief yet very clear definition of regeneration, which deeply impressed me. We may take this definition for granted, yet we have to realize that such a definition is profound. It is difficult to find such a word in any other Christian writings. We need to be impressed that through regeneration, we receive the divine life in addition to our natural, human life.

Regeneration is to have another birth, to be born of God. This is clearly revealed in John 1:13, which says that those who receive Christ are "begotten not of blood, nor of the will of the flesh, nor of the will of man, but of God." Whoever is regenerated is born of God. Regeneration is not a matter of considering that all things in the past are dead and that everything is new today. Regeneration is not a consideration but a real birth. Regeneration is to be born of God in order that we may have the divine life in addition to our human life.

I feel strongly that we need to impress the brothers and sisters that to be born again means to be born of God so that we may have a second life, a life in addition to our natural life.

Our natural life is a created life and a temporary life. It is not an eternal life and an uncreated life. In regeneration we receive another life, which is the eternal life, the uncreated life, the divine life, that is, the life of God. We must point this out clearly.

Some Christian teachers would say that to be born again is just to have a new beginning, a new day in your human life. This is not the truth of regeneration revealed in the Bible. Regeneration is a matter of birth, a matter of life. It is not a birth of the natural life, of the human life; it is the birth of the divine life, of the eternal life, the life of God. To be born again is to experience an extra birth of the life of God—the eternal, uncreated, divine life.

II. THE WAY

Now we want to see the way of regeneration.

A. To Realize Our Need of the Life of God

First, we need to realize our need of the life of God. This is related to God's eternal purpose. God's eternal purpose is to have a corporate people who can express Him. For these people to express God, they surely need the life and the nature of God. If we only have the human life, we can only express our human being. We cannot express God, the Divine Being. The particular life that something has issues in an expression. Dogs express the dog life, and cats express the cat life. An apple tree cannot express the life and nature of a peach tree, because it does not have the peach life and nature. For us human beings to express God, we need God's life. Genesis 1 shows us God's purpose for man to express Him, and in Genesis 2 we see the need for man to partake of the tree of life, the life of God. We have to realize that we need the life of God in order to express God.

A number of Bible teachers say that we need to be regenerated because we are fallen and sinful. This is a wrong concept. We have to tell people that even if man had never become fallen, he would still need regeneration. Even before man fell, he still needed the divine life. The very man whom God put in front of the tree of life was not fallen. He was pure, he was good, he was perfect, and he was sinless, but he was only human, not divine. Thus, Genesis 2 indicates clearly that this sinless man, perfect man, good man, and pure man, still needed the life of God. We need to be purged from the wrong, traditional concept that regeneration is because of man's fall. According to this concept, if man never fell, he would not have the need of regeneration. But the Bible reveals that regeneration is needed by man even if man never fell.

In order for one to be regenerated, he first has to realize his need of the divine life. In John 3:3 the Lord said, "Truly, truly, I say to you, Unless one is born anew, he cannot see the kingdom of God." In spiritual things to see is to enter into (v. 5). If you have not been born of God, you cannot enter into, or see, anything in the realm of God's kingdom. If you do not have the bird life, you cannot enter into the kingdom of the birds. If you do not have the animal life, you cannot enter into the kingdom of the animals. In order to enter into any kind of kingdom, you need that kind of life. If you do not have that kind of life, you can never get into that kingdom, that realm, or really understand what is within that realm.

If we did not have the human life, we could not be in the human kingdom, the kingdom of man. We have been born with the human life into the kingdom of man. Today we need to be born with the divine life into the kingdom of God. If we were only born of man, we could only be in man's kingdom. We could never be in the kingdom of God. To be in the kingdom of God, we need to be born of God, to be born again. John 3:3 shows the need of the life of God.

B. To Realize That Our Natural Being
Needs to Be Buried in the Water of Baptism

In order to be regenerated, we need to realize that our natural being needs to be buried in the water of baptism. In John 3:5 the Lord Jesus said, "Truly, truly, I say to you, Unless one is born of water and the Spirit, he cannot enter into the kingdom of God." When the Lord Jesus told Nicodemus that he needed to be born again, Nicodemus asked, "How can a man be born when he is old? He cannot enter a second time into his mother's womb and be born, can he?" (v. 4). Then the Lord explained to him that to be born again is to be born of water and of the Spirit.

John 3:5 has been altogether misinterpreted through the centuries by many teachers. One of the strangest teachings is that the water in this verse refers to the water of the mother's womb. But this is not the way to interpret the Bible. We need to interpret the Bible with and by the Bible. Nicodemus was a Pharisee. Before he came to the Lord, the Pharisees heard John the Baptist tell them, "I baptize you in water unto repentance, but He...will baptize you in the Holy Spirit" (Matt. 3:11). John told them that he came to baptize in water and that one after him would come to baptize in the Spirit. When the Lord was speaking to Nicodemus, He used the words *of water and the Spirit*. These words should have been familiar and plain to Nicodemus, without any need of explanation, since John the Baptist had spoken the same words to the Pharisees.

Water and *Spirit* actually refer to two ministries. *Water* refers to the water of baptism, the central concept of the ministry of John the Baptist, the ministry of repentance. John's ministry of repentance was to put people into the water, to bury people, to terminate people of the old creation. John baptized in water whoever came to him with repentance to terminate them for the purpose of their receiving Christ as the coming One who would put them into the Spirit of life. Thus, *water* refers to John's ministry, and *Spirit* refers to the Lord Jesus' ministry. Through these two ministries man is regenerated.

We not only need to realize that we need the life of God, but we also need to realize that our natural being should be terminated. In the New Testament usage, the word *repentance* means to realize that you are good only for being buried. You have been away from God, and now you have to have a turn to come back to Him. When you come back, when you have a turn, you have to be terminated, to be buried, to be put under the water. Following this burial comes resurrection, and this is of the Spirit. Water is for burial, for termination, and the Spirit is for being raised up from death, for germination. These two main concepts together constitute the concept of regeneration.

Regeneration is the termination of people of the old creation with their deeds and the germination of people in the new creation with the divine life. To be born of water is to be buried, to be terminated, and to be born of the Spirit is to be raised up from death to be resurrected, to be germinated. This is what it means to be born of God. Real regeneration is to be born of water and the Spirit, that is, to be terminated and buried in the water and to be germinated and resurrected with the Spirit to have another life.

C. To Be Born of the Spirit of God in Our Spirit

To be regenerated is to be born of the Spirit of God in our spirit (John 3:5, 6b). We are reborn not of earthly parents but of the Spirit of God, not in our body or in our soul but in our spirit. John 3:6b says, "That which is born of the Spirit is spirit." In other words, that which is born of the Spirit of God is our spirit. This indicates that regeneration is the rebirth of the Spirit, which transpires in our spirit. Regeneration is accomplished in the human spirit by the Holy Spirit with God's life— the uncreated, eternal life. It is altogether a matter of the divine Spirit in our human spirit.

We need to make these things clear to all the saints. I do not have much confidence that even those who have been with us for years are clear about these things. We need a basic training so that we can be saturated with this basic knowledge. We need to realize that we have been born again of the Spirit of God in our spirit. This is the very basic and foundational truth concerning regeneration.

1. By Believing into the Son of God

We are born of the Spirit of God in our spirit by believing into the Son of God. John 3:36a says, "He who believes into the Son has eternal life."

2. Through the Word of God in the Gospel

Our being born of the Spirit of God in our spirit is through the word of God in the gospel. We have to receive the word of the gospel. When we believe in the Lord Jesus, it is through the word of God in the gospel that we are regenerated. First Peter 1:23 says that we were regenerated through the living and abiding word of God. James 1:18 says that He brought us forth by the word of truth. Finally, in 1 Corinthians 4:15 Paul says, "I have begotten you through the gospel." Thus, the word of God in the gospel is the seed of our rebirth.

III. THE ISSUE

Now that we have seen the way to be regenerated, we want to see the issue of regeneration.

A. Resurrected with Christ

The first issue of regeneration is that we are resurrected with Christ. First Peter 1:3b says that we were regenerated through the resurrection of Christ. Ephesians 2:5a says that God made us alive together with Christ. When Christ was resurrected, we were also resurrected with Him. From God's viewpoint we were resurrected together with Christ and regenerated through His resurrection. But this is realized by us experientially and applied to us when we are regenerated in time. Thus, the result of our regeneration is that we are resurrected with Christ.

B. Having the Eternal and Uncreated Life

When we were regenerated, God put His eternal and uncreated life into our being (1 John 1:2).

C. Becoming a Child of God

Since God has put His life into us, we have become children of God. John 1:12 says that we have the authority to be the children of God. This authority is the life that God put into us. The very life that God put into us is our right, our authority, for us to be children of God.

D. Partaking of the Divine Nature

Regeneration results in the partaking of God's divine nature. Because we are born of God, surely as His children we have not only His life but also His nature. Second Peter 1:4 says that we are partakers of the divine nature.

E. Born into the Kingdom of God

Since we are born of God, spontaneously we are born into

the realm of God, into the sphere of God, that is, into the king-dom of God (John 3:5). This is the result, the issue, of our regeneration.

We need to emphasize the focus of this lesson, which is expressed in the following statement: to be regenerated is to have the life of God so that we may be His children living in His kingdom according to His divine nature.

THE WASHING OF REGENERATION
AND
THE RENEWING OF THE HOLY SPIRIT

Scripture Reading: Titus 3:5; 2 Cor. 5:17; Ezek. 36:26-27a;
2 Cor. 3:18; Rom. 12:2a; Col. 3:10

OUTLINE

I. The washing of regeneration:
  A. Regeneration being a change of position—a new state of things—cf. Matt. 19:28.
  B. Washing being the laver to purge away the old things of our natural life on the negative side—2 Cor. 5:17:
    1. Organically.
    2. Metabolically.
II. The renewing of the Holy Spirit:
  A. To reconstitute our being on the positive side:
    1. With the divine life—John 1:13b; 3:5b.
    2. With the divine nature—2 Pet. 1:4.
    3. By renewing our heart.
    4. By renewing our spirit—Ezek. 36:26.
  B. To transform us—2 Cor. 3:18:
    1. By dwelling in us—Ezek. 36:27a; Rom. 8:9, 11.
    2. By renewing our soul—12:2a.
    3. By renewing the new man unto full knowledge according to the image of God—Col. 3:10.

Focus: The washing of regeneration is to purge away the old things of our natural life, and the renewing of the Holy Spirit is to reconstitute us and transform us with the divine life and the divine nature into the image of God.

In this lesson we want to see the washing of regeneration and the renewing of the Holy Spirit spoken of in Titus 3:5.

I. THE WASHING OF REGENERATION

A. Regeneration Being a Change of Position— a New State of Things

The Greek word for *regeneration* in Titus 3:5 is different from that for *regenerated* in 1 Peter 1:23. The only other place the word is used is in Matthew 19:28, where it is used for the restoration in the millennium. Regeneration in Titus 3:5 is a change of position, a new state of things. When a person is reborn, the divine life gets into him. Then there is a change of position, and the state of things becomes new. Titus 3:5 speaks of the washing of a changed position, a state of things that has become new. Being born again is the commencing of a change from one state to another.

B. Washing Being the Laver to Purge Away the Old Things of Our Natural Life on the Negative Side

Titus 3:5 speaks of the "washing of regeneration." The Greek word for *washing* here is literally *laver*. The same word is used in Ephesians 5:26 for *washing*—"the washing of the water in the word." The laver of the Old Testament tabernacle was for the washing away of uncleanness. The washing of regeneration is a laver to purge away the old things of our natural life on the negative side. Second Corinthians 5:17 says, "If anyone is in Christ, he is a new creation. The old things have passed away; behold, they have become new." Everything of our natural life is old. These old things of our natural life are purged away by the washing, the laver, of a changed position and of a new state of things.

This washing is organic, not something of doctrinal knowledge, outward correction, or outward regulation. The washing of regeneration is altogether related to another life that enters into our being organically. If a person swallowed a pearl, it would enter into his being in an inorganic way because the pearl does not possess any element of life. But when a person eats nourishing food, the food is digested and assimilated by him. The food gets into his being as his life supply in an organic way, and it even becomes the constituents of the tissues of his physical being. Food gets into us organically. It is absolutely related to life. The washing of regeneration, of the changed position and new state of things, is also absolutely in life and with life. It is an organic, inward washing in life that carries away all the negative things, purging away all the things of the old nature of our old man.

Furthermore, this washing is metabolic because it imparts something new into us, and the new things of the divine life replace the old things of our natural life. In the metabolism of our physical body, the old, negative things are carried away and replaced with the new supply of life so that we may be strengthened and grow. The washing of regeneration is also a metabolic process, a metabolic washing, in which the old, negative things of our natural life are carried away and replaced with the new things of the divine life for our supply and growth in the divine life.

II. THE RENEWING OF THE HOLY SPIRIT

A. To Reconstitute Our Being on the Positive Side

The washing is mainly to purge away the old things of our natural life on the negative side, and the renewing of the Holy Spirit is to reconstitute our being on the positive side. Something new, real, and solid of the divine life is being carried into our being to renew our old life.

The renewing of the Holy Spirit is always with the divine life. John 1:13b says that we are begotten of God, and 3:5b says that we are born of the Spirit. To be born of God, to be born of the Spirit, is to have the divine life imparted into our being. The divine life is now the renewing element in our being. The Holy Spirit renews our being with such a solid element, that is, the divine life. The Holy Spirit renews us not only with the divine life but also with the divine nature. Second Peter 1:4 says that we are partakers of the divine nature. The divine life and the divine nature are the elements of the renewing of the Holy Spirit.

We also need to point out that the Holy Spirit renews us by renewing our heart and by renewing our spirit. Ezekiel 36:26 says that God gives us a new heart and puts a new spirit within us. Actually, the new heart and the new spirit are the renewed heart and the renewed spirit. This may be compared to the old heaven and old earth being renewed to be the new heaven and new earth. Our old being is being renewed into a new being. At the time of our rebirth, God gave us a new heart and a new spirit. In other words, He renewed our heart and our spirit by the Spirit.

The heart is a loving organ, and the spirit is a receiving organ. We love God with our heart and receive God with our spirit. But both our spirit and our heart were old and were not fulfilling their proper functions. In our new birth the Spirit of God renewed our heart to love God and renewed our spirit to receive God. This is fully proven by our experience. We can testify that when we were born again, we began to love God, and we longed to receive God by contacting Him in our spirit.

B. To Transform Us

The renewing of the Holy Spirit is not just to reconstitute our being on the positive side but also to transform us. Second Corinthians 3:18 says, "We all with unveiled face, beholding and reflecting like a mirror the glory of the Lord, are being transformed into the same image from glory to glory, even as from the Lord Spirit."

The Holy Spirit transforms us first by dwelling in us. Ezekiel 36:27a says that besides giving us a new heart and putting in us a new spirit, God also put His own Spirit into our being. Romans 8:9 and 11 show that the Spirit of God dwells in us to saturate our being with the divine, resurrection life.

The Holy Spirit dwells in us in order to transform us by renewing our soul. Romans 12:2a says that we are to be transformed by the renewing of our mind. This means that the indwelling Spirit of God renews our soul, comprising our mind, our emotion, and our will.

Furthermore, according to Colossians 3:10, the Holy Spirit transforms us by renewing the new man unto full knowledge according to the image of God, the One who created him. This means that the indwelling Spirit of God renews us day by day unto the full knowledge of God according to what God is, according to the image of God. The renewing work of the Holy Spirit is making all of us a part of the renewed new man so that the new man may resemble God in full. The new man is the Body of Christ, the church. We have to stress emphatically that the renewing of the Holy Spirit eventually consummates in making us absolutely in the image of God in full.

The focus of this lesson may be expressed in the following statement: the washing of regeneration is to purge away the old things of our natural life, and the renewing of the Holy Spirit is to reconstitute us and transform us with the divine life and the divine nature into the image of God. This makes us the same as God is, not in an individual way but in a corporate way.

THE FELLOWSHIP OF LIFE

Scripture Reading: 1 John 1:2-3, 5-7, 9; 1 Cor. 10:16; 2 Cor. 13:14; Phil. 2:1; John 15:4-5; Philem. 6

OUTLINE

I. The meaning of the fellowship of life:
   A. Sharing in common—1 Cor. 10:16; Philem. 6.
   B. The flowing of the divine life within us—1 John 1:2-3, 6-7:
      1. Vertically between the Father, the Son, and us— v. 6.
      2. Horizontally between us and one another—v. 7.
II. The source of the fellowship of life—the eternal life of God—vv. 2-3.
III. The means of the fellowship of life—the Holy Spirit— 2 Cor. 13:14.
IV. The location of the fellowship of life—our spirit—Phil. 2:1.
V. The function of the fellowship of life—supplying us with all the riches of the divine life—John 15:4-5.
VI. The issue of the fellowship of life:
   A. Bringing light to us—1 John 1:5-7.
   B. Bringing the practical cleansing of the blood to us—v. 7.
   C. Keeping us abiding in the Lord—John 15:4-5.
VII. The relationship between the fellowship of life and the sense of life:
   A. The fellowship of life being realized by the sense of life.
   B. The sense of life preserving the fellowship of life.

VIII. The breaking of the fellowship of life:
 A. By sins.
 B. By disobedience.
 C. By not caring for the sense of life.
 D. By not following the inner anointing—1 John 2:27.
 IX. The restoration of the fellowship of life:
 A. By the confessing of our sins—1:9.
 B. By the cleansing of the blood.

Focus: The fellowship of life, being the flowing of the divine life, comes from the life of God and is preserved by the sense of life to supply us with the riches of the divine life.

In this lesson we want to see something concerning the fellowship of life. The King James Version renders the word *fellowship* as "communion." "Communion" is a good translation, but its true meaning has been somewhat spoiled by traditional thought and usage.

In Philippians 2:1 the apostle Paul speaks of the fellowship of spirit. A number of translators consider that the spirit mentioned here is the Spirit of God. But actually this is not the Spirit of God but our spirit. We know this because it is mentioned in the context of a list of our spiritual virtues. In Philippians 2:1 Paul speaks of encouragement in Christ, consolation of love, fellowship of spirit, and tenderheartedness and compassions. These are not the virtues of God but our spiritual virtues, so the spirit here must be our spirit. We have to make this point clear to the saints. This is very important because this verse tells us that the fellowship of life is going on in our spirit. Our spirit is the location of today's fellowship that we have with the Lord and with the saints.

In John 15:4-5 the word *fellowship* is not mentioned, but we know that these verses in fact refer to the fellowship. In these two verses the word used to indicate fellowship is *abide*. The Lord said, "Abide in Me and I in you." This mutual abiding actually is the fellowship.

I. THE MEANING OF THE FELLOWSHIP OF LIFE

A. Sharing in Common

In Greek the word for *fellowship* means "sharing in common." First Corinthians 10:16 says, "The cup of blessing which we bless, is it not the fellowship of the blood of Christ? The bread which we break, is it not the fellowship of the body of Christ?" We share the Lord's Body in common, and we share the cup in common, so the Body and the cup become our fellowship. In Philemon 6 Paul speaks of "the fellowship of your faith." Philemon had faith and with that faith there was a kind of sharing in common.

B. The Flowing of the Divine Life within Us

The fellowship of life is the flowing of the divine life within us (1 John 1:2-3, 6-7). We can illustrate this with two things. First, the circulation of blood is a very good illustration of the flowing of life. The blood within our physical body flows, circulates, all the time, and this circulating, or this flowing, is a good picture of the spiritual fellowship of life, the flowing of the divine life. Another illustration that can be used is the current of electricity. The current of electricity is the moving of electricity. In like manner, the fellowship of life is the moving, the flowing, of the divine life within us. We all know that the blood circulation needs the vessels of our body, and the electrical current needs the wires. We are like the vessels and the wires for the spiritual flow of the divine life.

1. Vertically between the Father, the Son, and Us

The flowing of the divine life within us first is vertical between the Father, the Son, and us (vv. 6, 3).

2. Horizontally between Us and One Another

The flowing of the divine life, the fellowship of life, is also horizontally between us and one another (v. 7). The horizontal aspect depends upon the vertical aspect. First John 1 says that we first have fellowship with the Father and the Son; then we have this fellowship with one another. If our fellowship is wrong vertically with the Father and the Son, we cannot have the fellowship horizontally with one another. The fellowship between us horizontally depends upon our fellowship with the Father and the Son vertically.

This vertical and horizontal fellowship is like the weaving of a textile. In this vertical and horizontal fellowship, there is the mingling of the Triune God—the Father, the Son, and the Spirit—with all the saints. Actually, the proper fellowship is the mingling of the Triune God with all the redeemed saints. In other words, the fellowship eventually consummates in the oneness of the Triune God with the Body of Christ. This fellowship is the flow of the life of the Triune God within us.

II. THE SOURCE OF THE FELLOWSHIP OF LIFE— THE ETERNAL LIFE OF GOD

The source of the fellowship of life is the eternal life of God.

First John 1:2-3 says that the eternal life has been reported to us so that we may have fellowship. This word proves that the fellowship comes out of the eternal life. The eternal life is the source of this fellowship. Just as the electrical current comes out of the power plant, the fellowship comes out of the eternal life.

Many in Christianity think that fellowship is a kind of social contact in a social association with social activities. But fellowship is not a kind of social contact. We have to reject that. We do not want that. The real and genuine fellowship among us originates in the eternal, divine life. If the source is wrong, that is not the genuine fellowship.

III. THE MEANS OF THE FELLOWSHIP OF LIFE— THE HOLY SPIRIT

The means by which the fellowship of life is carried out is the Holy Spirit, so it is called the fellowship of the Holy Spirit in 2 Corinthians 13:14. The Holy Spirit is the instrument, the means, that carries out this fellowship. Actually, it is really hard for us in our experience to differentiate these three things: the fellowship, the life, and the Spirit. These three things are one. The life is the source, the fellowship is the flow, and the Spirit is the carrier, the means. In our experience we cannot differentiate them, but in our explanation of the truth we can.

IV. THE LOCATION OF THE FELLOWSHIP OF LIFE— OUR SPIRIT

Our spirit is the location of the fellowship of life. This is based upon Philippians 2:1. We have to point out as clearly and strongly as possible that if our contact with one another is not in the spirit, right away it becomes a social thing. Our contact must be in the spirit. Then our contact becomes the fellowship. This is because the flowing of the divine life is altogether not in our soul, our natural life. It is altogether in our spirit.

The fellowship of life is carried out by God's Spirit in our spirit. Our mind may apprehend the fellowship, but it is not in our mind. Our emotions may be happy about it, but the fellowship of life is not in our emotion. It is altogether in our spirit. So if we are apart from our spirit or outside of our spirit, right away our contact with one another becomes a kind of social association that is no longer the fellowship of life. The fellowship of life must be in our spirit.

V. THE FUNCTION OF THE FELLOWSHIP OF LIFE— SUPPLYING US WITH ALL THE RICHES OF THE DIVINE LIFE

If the fellowship of life did not have a function, it would be meaningless. The function of the fellowship of life is to supply us with all the riches of the divine life (John 15:4-5). The more the divine life flows within us, the more supply of life it carries to us. A good picture of this is the flowing of the river of water of life in the New Jerusalem (Rev. 22:1-2). In that river is the tree of life. The tree of life indicates the supply that goes along with the flowing of the river of water of life, which is the fellowship of life. Thus, the tree of life going along with the river indicates the function of the flowing of the river of life. This function is to supply us with the riches of the divine life.

John 15:4-5 says that we abide in the vine, and then the vine abides in us. This abiding supplies us with the life-juice of the vine. We know this because our abiding eventually issues in fruit-bearing. The fruit-bearing proves that the abiding supplies us with the rich life of the vine tree. The fellowship of life functions in this unique thing—to supply us with the riches of the life of Christ.

VI. THE ISSUE OF THE FELLOWSHIP OF LIFE

A. Bringing Light to Us

The first issue of the fellowship of life is that it brings light to us (1 John 1:5-7). God is light, and if we have fellowship with Him, we are in the light.

B. Bringing the Practical Cleansing of the Blood to Us

The fellowship of life not only brings light to us but also brings the practical cleansing of the blood to us. The blood's cleansing might be a mere doctrine and an objective fact to us. It may be there doctrinally as a fact, but it has nothing to do with us until we are really in the fellowship. First John 1:7 says that when we are in the light, we have fellowship, and the blood cleanses us. If we are not in the fellowship, we may say that we apply the blood and we may believe that the blood cleanses us, but actually the cleansing is not there. The blood actually cleanses us and is applied to us when we are really in the fellowship. This point is quite crucial.

Many Christians believe that the blood cleanses them, but this cleansing is not practically applied to them because they are not in the fellowship. The blood does not practically cleanse us outside the fellowship. We must be in the fellowship. There is only one verse in the whole Bible that tells us how the cleansing can be practical. That verse is 1 John 1:7. It says that when we are in the light, we have fellowship with one another, and the blood of Jesus cleanses us from every sin.

C. Keeping Us Abiding in the Lord

The issue of the fellowship is that it keeps us abiding in the Lord (John 15:4-5). Actually, the abiding is the fellowship, and the fellowship is the abiding.

VII. THE RELATIONSHIP BETWEEN
THE FELLOWSHIP OF LIFE AND THE SENSE OF LIFE

A. The Fellowship of Life
Being Realized by the Sense of Life

If we do not have the sense of life, we cannot realize the fellowship of life. The fellowship of life is known, sensed, realized, by the sense of life. How can we know that we have the fellowship of life, the flow of the divine life, within us? It is by the sense of life. We can illustrate this with our physical body. When our physical body has no illness, no problem, we do not have any feeling, but when we are ill, we are full of feeling. When we feel something in our stomach, this means that we have stomach trouble. When we do not feel anything, this means that our stomach is okay. It is the same with the fellowship of life.

Usually, when we have the fellowship of life, we do not feel that much, but when there is something wrong with the fellowship of life, the flowing of the divine life, we sense it. If we are walking in the light, in the fellowship of life, we do not have any special sensation. When we have a negative and abnormal sensation, that proves we have the fellowship of life, but it also proves that something is wrong with the fellowship of life. Thus, the fellowship of life is realized by the sense of life.

B. The Sense of Life
Preserving the Fellowship of Life

The fellowship of life is preserved, safeguarded, protected, by the sense of life. With our physical body it is the same. Our feelings of pain or discomfort are a protection and a safeguard to us. Thus, to realize the fellowship of life and to safeguard, keep, and preserve the fellowship of life are all by the sense of life.

VIII. THE BREAKING OF THE FELLOWSHIP OF LIFE

Our relationship of life with the Father can never be broken, but the fellowship can be broken. The breaking of the fellowship of life is like the breaking of the electrical current. Even a small thing can cut off the electricity, and this breaks the electrical current.

A. By Sins

The breaking of the fellowship of life is first by sins. If we do something that we know is sinful, this breaks, cuts off, the fellowship of life.

B. By Disobedience

If we disobey God, this surely cuts off the fellowship of life.

C. By Not Caring for the Sense of Life

We must care for the sense of life. If we do not care for it, this will break the fellowship of life.

D. By Not Following the Inner Anointing

The main things that generally cut off the fellowship of life are sins, disobedience, not caring for the sense of life, and not following the inner anointing. First John 2:27 says clearly that we have to abide in the Lord according to the teaching of the anointing.

IX. THE RESTORATION OF THE FELLOWSHIP OF LIFE

After the fellowship of life is broken, we have to restore it.

A. By the Confessing of Our Sins

We have to confess our sins. First John 1:9 says that if we confess our sins, God is faithful and righteous to forgive us our sins and cleanse us from all unrighteousness. He forgives us according to His word faithfully and also according to the redemptive work of Christ righteously. Thus, by confessing our sins, our broken fellowship of life can surely be restored.

B. By the Cleansing of the Blood

The confessing is on our side, and the cleansing is on God's side. If we confess, surely the blood cleanses us, and the broken fellowship is always restored.

The focus of this lesson is as follows: the fellowship of life, being the flowing of the divine life, comes from the life of God and is preserved by the sense of life to supply us with the riches of the divine life.

THE SENSE OF LIFE

Scripture Reading: Rom. 8:6, 2, 11; Eph. 4:18-19; Heb. 8:10;
1 John 2:27; John 15:4-5; Phil. 2:13

OUTLINE

I. The meaning of the sense of life:
   A. The feeling of death—weakness, emptiness, uneasiness, restlessness, depression, dryness, darkness, pain, etc.—on the negative side—Rom. 8:6a.
   B. The feeling of life and peace—strength, satisfaction, peace, rest, release, liveliness, watering, brightness, comfort, etc.—on the positive side—v. 6b.
   C. Related to the consciousness of the conscience—Eph. 4:19.

II. The source of the sense of life:
   A. The divine life with the richest, strongest, and keenest feeling—Eph. 4:18.
   B. The law of life—the natural ability and function of life—Rom. 8:2; Heb. 8:10.
   C. The Holy Spirit—the anointing ointment—Rom. 8:11; 1 John 2:27.
   D. Christ abiding in us—John 15:4-5.
   E. God operating in us—Phil. 2:13.

III. The function of the sense of life:
   A. Making us know whether we are living in the natural life or in the divine life.
   B. Making us know whether we are living in the flesh or in the spirit.

Now that we have seen something concerning the fellowship of life, we want to go on to see the sense of life. We saw in the previous lesson that the fellowship of life is realized by the sense of life and that the sense of life preserves the fellowship of life.

Romans 8:6 says that the mind set on the flesh is death, but the mind set on the spirit is life and peace. Verse 2 of Romans 8 speaks of the law of the Spirit of life, and verse 11 speaks of the Spirit who dwells in us. Then we have to read Ephesians 4:18-19. In verse 18 there is the life of God. The unbelievers are alienated from the life of God. Then verse 19 says that they are "past feeling." Hebrews 8:10 says that in the new covenant God writes His laws within the believers. Then 1 John 2:27 speaks concerning the anointing that teaches the believers concerning all things. John 15:4-5 speaks of our mutual abiding with the Lord, and Philippians 2:13 speaks of God operating in us both the willing and the working for His good pleasure. These are some of the most precious verses in the New Testament, and they all have something to do with the sense of life. Of course, in the whole New Testament you cannot find a verse that directly uses the term *the sense of life*. But the sense of life is thoroughly implied and referred to in all the above verses.

I. THE MEANING OF THE SENSE OF LIFE

First, we need to see the meaning, the definition, of the sense of life.

A. The Feeling of Death—
Weakness, Emptiness, Uneasiness, Restlessness,
Depression, Dryness, Darkness, Pain, Etc.—
on the Negative Side

The sense of life on the negative side is the feeling of death, a kind of negative feeling. This is definitely revealed in Romans 8:6. We have to realize that Romans 8:6 is altogether a verse of sensation because it says that the mind set on the flesh is death. This is not only a fact, but it is also a matter of feeling, a matter of consciousness. When you set your mind on the flesh, you have the sense of death. You feel that death is there.

The feeling of death is the inner feeling of weakness, emptiness, uneasiness, restlessness, depression, dryness, darkness, pain, etc.—on the negative side (v. 6a). When you sense that you are weak, empty, uneasy, restless, depressed, dried up, darkened, and in pain within, this indicates that death is there. When death is present, this means that you have set your mind on the flesh. To set the mind on the flesh simply means to live in the flesh. The mind is the key of our daily walk. The key opens the gate for us to walk on the way. To set the mind on the flesh simply means to open the gate of the flesh and to walk the fleshly way. Thus, when you sense that death is present, you have to realize that you are living, walking, in the flesh. This is the negative function of the sense of life.

B. The Feeling of Life and Peace—
Strength, Satisfaction, Peace, Rest, Release, Liveliness, Watering, Brightness, Comfort, Etc.— on the Positive Side

On the positive side the sense of life functions to give us a consciousness of the following positive things—strength, satisfaction, peace, rest, release, liveliness, watering, brightness, comfort, etc. (v. 6b). Instead of being weak, we are strong. Instead of being empty, we are satisfied. Instead of uneasiness and restlessness, we have peace and rest. Instead of depression, we have release and liveliness. Liveliness is a kind of condition of livingness. We have a sense of watering versus dryness, brightness versus darkness, and comfort versus pain. All these are the positive feelings we have from the function of the sense of life. When we have these kinds of feelings, we have to realize that this is the working of the sense of life.

Thus, in Romans 8:6 the main thing that is implied is the sense of life. To set the mind on the spirit is life and peace. This is altogether a matter of sensation and consciousness. This consciousness is the sense of life. It functions not only to guide us but also to govern us, to control us, and to direct us. The feeling of death and the feeling of life and peace are the two aspects of the meaning of the sense of life.

C. Related to the Consciousness
of the Conscience

On both the negative side and the positive side, the sense of life is always related to the consciousness of the conscience. Ephesians 4:19 says that the unbelievers are "past feeling." *Feeling* here refers mainly to the consciousness of one's conscience. The unbelievers in general do not care for the feeling of their conscience. The most careless people concerning their inner feeling are the most sinful people. The unbelievers who endeavor to be good persons surely would take care of their inner feeling. Just to be governed by the law, by the police, is not up to the moral standard. Even with the unbelievers, the moral standard must be according to the inner feeling of their conscience. Of course, the sense of life, for a believer, is not simply a matter of the conscience, but it is related to the consciousness of the conscience according to the sense of life, the life of God.

II. THE SOURCE OF THE SENSE OF LIFE

A. The Divine Life with the Richest,
Strongest, and Keenest Feeling

Any kind of life has its feeling. If something does not have any feeling, it has no life. It is a dead thing. A stone does not have any feeling, but anything that has life has feeling. The higher the life is, the stronger the feeling is. The divine life is the strongest and highest life, so it has the richest, strongest, and keenest feeling (v. 18). The divine life is the first item of the source of the sense of life. According to Ephesians 4:18-19, the unbelievers are past feeling because they are alienated from the life of God. If we are one with the life of God, we will have the richest, strongest, and keenest feeling.

B. The Law of Life—
the Natural Ability and Function of Life

The law of life is the natural ability and function of life (Rom. 8:2; Heb. 8:10) and is another item of the source of life. Because this life-law functions within us, it surely gives us a certain kind of sensation, so it is an aspect of the source of life.

Romans 8:2 speaks of the law of the Spirit of life, and Hebrews 8:10 says that this law is inscribed on our hearts.

C. The Holy Spirit—the Anointing Oil

The Holy Spirit—the anointing oil—is also an aspect of the source of the sense of life (Rom. 8:11; 1 John 2:27). Exodus 30 speaks of the anointing oil, the compound ointment for the tabernacle and the priesthood. In ancient times, the tabernacle with all its utensils and the priests were anointed with the ointment. Today the Holy Spirit is the ointment to the whole church with all the saints. The Spirit anoints us continuously, and His anointing is a kind of inner working and moving that gives us the sense of life. This anointing Spirit is also the source of the sense of life.

D. Christ Abiding in Us

Christ abiding in us is another aspect of the source of the sense of life (John 15:4-5). Actually, His abiding in us is the function of life and gives us the sense of life.

E. God Operating in Us

God is operating in us all the time (Phil. 2:13). His inner operation gives us the sense of life. Thus, it is a source of the sense of life.

Regardless of how moral the unbelievers are, they have only the human conscience to go by, and this has been greatly damaged by the fall of man. Even today with many unbelievers, their conscience has been damaged and even seared by their daily sinfulness. Their damaged conscience does not work very well. Even if the unbelievers' conscience did work well, it is the only thing that they have.

The teaching of Confucius is altogether centered on the developing of the conscience, which is referred to by him as the "bright virtue." His ethical teachings and the positive teachings of the good philosophers are focused on the development of the human conscience. The development of the goodness within a person is the development of his conscience, which was created by God.

The unbelievers have the human conscience, but we believers

have not only a created conscience but also a renewed conscience. Our conscience, as a part of our spirit (Rom. 9:1; cf. 8:16), has been renewed through the regeneration of our spirit. In addition to this renewed conscience we have these five great things: the divine life, the law of the divine life, the Holy Spirit, Christ, and God. Thus, there is no comparison between the created conscience of the unbelievers and the renewed conscience of the believers who are indwelt by the Triune God as the divine life.

We Christians should be persons full of feeling all the time. We should not be dull or numb. We must be very sensitive, full of sensations because we are living and rich in life. This is because we have a regenerated spirit with our conscience renewed. We also have the divine life, the law of this divine life, the Holy Spirit, Christ, and God. Therefore the sense of life is high, rich, strong, and keen within us.

III. THE FUNCTION OF THE SENSE OF LIFE

Now we want to see the function of the sense of life.

A. Making Us Know Whether We Are Living in the Natural Life or in the Divine Life

If we are living in the natural life, the sense is of death and is entirely on the negative side. Then we have the feeling of death with all of its negative points. If we are living in the divine life, the sense is of life and is entirely on the positive side. Then we have the feeling of life and peace with all of its positive points. The sense of life makes us know whether we are living in the natural life or in the divine life. The sense of life guides us, governs us, controls us, and directs us. This truth has been altogether lost in today's Christianity. Most of the teachings of today's Christianity are focused on morality and good behavior. They do not care for this inner sense of life functioning to make us know whether we are living in the natural life or in the divine life. Since we are seeking after Christ as our life, we must take care of this sense of life. If we do not have the positive sensations of strength, satisfaction, peace, rest, release, liveliness, watering, brightness, comfort, etc., we must realize that we are not living in the divine life; it must be that we are living in the natural life.

B. Making Us Know Whether We Are Living in the Flesh or in the Spirit

The function of the sense of life is also to make us know whether we are living in the natural life or in the divine life. To live in the natural life is one thing, and to live in the flesh is another thing. You may consider that these are one, but still there is a little difference. The flesh is always bad. There is no good flesh. But the natural life sometimes may be good. The natural life is versus the divine life, and the flesh is versus the spirit.

Therefore, there are two aspects concerning the function of the sense of life. The first aspect is to let you know whether you are living in the divine life, and the second aspect is to let you know whether you are living in your spirit. Negatively speaking, it makes you know whether you are living in the natural life, as a natural person, and also whether you are living in the flesh. In our experience we always can differentiate these two things. Many times we have the sense that we are living, walking, and acting in the flesh. Sometimes we are not that fleshly, but still we have the sense that we are walking in our natural life, in our natural man, not in the divine life.

Before we speak this lesson to the saints, we need much prayer to get into these points. This lesson should not be a mere doctrine of knowledge according to the letter. It must be something of life from our experience. We need much prayer to pray ourselves into the sense of life. Then we can give a word not merely in teaching but practically in fellowship. Our message will be a kind of fellowship, telling people how we have experienced these things, how the sense of life is so real and practical to us, and how we are under this kind of controlling, guiding, directing element within us day by day.

THE DISPENSING FUNCTION
OF THE TRIUNE GOD

Scripture Reading: Rom. 8:9-11, 14, 16; Eph. 3:14, 16-17a, 19b; 4:6; John 15:1, 5, 26; 14:10, 17-20, 23; Heb. 8:10-11; 1 John 2:27

OUTLINE

   I. God the Father:
      A. Being the source—John 15:1b; Eph. 3:14, 16a.
      B. Abiding in us—Eph. 4:6.
  II. God the Son:
      A. Being the embodiment of the Father—John 15:1a; 14:10.
      B. Abiding in us and making His home in our hearts—15:4a; Eph. 3:17a.
 III. God the Spirit:
      A. The reality of the Son—John 14:17-20.
      B. Dwelling in us—Rom. 8:11.
 IV. The Triune God—the Father, the Son, and the Spirit—dispensing Himself into our being—Eph. 3:14, 16-17a, 19b.
  V. The dispensing function of the Triune God issuing in the sense of life:
      A. Through the law of life—Heb. 8:10-11.
      B. By the teaching of the anointing—1 John 2:27.
      C. In our spirit mingled with the life-giving Spirit—Rom. 8:16, 14.

Now that we have seen something concerning the sense of life, we need to go on to see the dispensing function of the Triune God.

Once in 1933 or 1934, Brother Watchman Nee spoke with me concerning the basic truths. At that time I did not see the Divine Trinity in His dispensing of Himself into our being. In my talk with Brother Nee, a number of times I did not refer to the Lord Jesus or Christ. I mostly used the title *God*. Brother Watchman Nee frankly told me that to merely use the title *God* is something according to the Old Testament. The orthodox Jews use the title *God*, but they do not refer to the Lord Jesus or to Christ in their worship.

At another time Brother Nee pointed out to me that the Catholic Church is a mixture of the New Testament with the Old Testament. What they practice in the Catholic Church in their services, their masses, is mostly according to the Old Testament forms, ordinances, and rituals. The priests in the Catholic Church burn incense and wear the priestly robes according to the practice of the Old Testament, yet they presume that they are practicing a New Testament service. Catholicism has this mixture also in their teaching. They do not discern the New Testament teaching from the Old Testament. The teaching of the Seventh-day Adventists is similar in the sense that their teaching is nearly altogether according to the Old Testament.

We need to be fully transferred out of all mixture into the pure New Testament revelation of the divine dispensing of the Divine Trinity. Romans 8:9-11 unveils the dispensing of the Triune God absolutely according to God's New Testament economy. These verses refer to the Spirit of God, the Spirit of Christ, and Christ Himself. This indicates that Christ is the Spirit of Christ and that the Spirit of Christ is the Spirit of God. Verse 10 says that Christ is in us, and verse 9 says that the Spirit dwells in us. The Greek word for *dwells* here means "to make home," or "reside."

God can dwell in us only through His Trinity. Without being the Triune God—the Father, the Son, and the Spirit—God cannot dwell in us. Eventually, the New Testament strongly tells us that it is the Spirit who dwells in us, who inhabits us.

The sense of life actually is the issue of the dispensing function of the Triune God. Because the Triune God is dispensing Himself into our being, we have the sense of life within us.

Very few Bible readers have seen the dispensing function of the Triune God in Romans 8:9-11. Verse 9 says, "You are not in the flesh, but in the spirit, if indeed the Spirit of God dwells in you." In verses 7 and 8 God is mentioned, but in verse 9 we see that it is the Spirit of God who dwells in us. Verse 9 continues, "Yet if anyone does not have the Spirit of Christ, he is not of Him." *The Spirit of Christ* is interchangeably used with *the Spirit of God*. Thus, the Spirit of God is the Spirit of Christ.

Verse 10 continues, "If Christ is in you, though the body is dead because of sin, the spirit is life because of righteousness." This shows that the Spirit of Christ is just Christ Himself. Verse 11 says, "If the Spirit of the One who raised Jesus from the dead dwells in you, He who raised Christ from the dead will also give life to your mortal bodies through His Spirit who indwells you." The Spirit of the resurrecting One, the One who raised Jesus from the dead, dwells in us. This is the Divine Trinity not only functioning but also dispensing.

Romans 8:10 says that our spirit is life; verse 6 says that our mind can be life; verse 11 goes on to say that this very life can be dispensed into our mortal body. This is the Triune God dispensing Himself as life into our whole being—the spirit, the mind, and the body. He gives life to our mortal body through His Spirit who indwells us. The entire Divine Trinity—the Father, the Son, and the Spirit—functions together to dispense Himself as life into our being. This is the dispensing function of the Triune God to dispense Himself as life into His believers.

In these verses we can see the Triune God dispensing Himself into the tripartite man. First, He dispenses Himself into our spirit and then from our spirit into our mind. If we set our mind upon the spirit, the life in the spirit will get into our mind. To set the mind on the spirit is life. Eventually, even the Spirit of Christ, the Spirit of God, God Himself, dwells in us to spread His life, to give His life, to our mortal body. This dispensing function issues in the sense of life.

In Ephesians 3:14-17 we can also see the dispensing function of the Divine Trinity. In these verses Paul says, "I bow my knees unto the Father...that He would grant you...to be strengthened with power through His Spirit into the inner man, that Christ may make His home in your hearts." Here the apostle Paul prays to the Father, the saints are strengthened into the inner man through the Spirit, and Christ makes His home in their hearts. The Father receives and answers the prayer, the Spirit strengthens, and then Christ makes His home in our hearts. The Triune God functions for the purpose of dispensing Himself into our being. When Christ makes His home in our hearts, our whole being will be taken over, possessed, occupied, and filled up with the Triune God.

Another portion concerning the dispensing function of the Triune God is in John 15. In verse 1 the Lord said, "I am the true vine, and My Father is the husbandman." The husbandman is the source, and the vine is the organism and the embodiment of what the source is, what the source has, and what the source does. In other words, whatever the Father is, has, and does is altogether embodied in this universal organism, the vine. The source is the Father, and the organism is the Son.

Both the source and the organism are made real by the Spirit of reality. In verse 26 of the same chapter the Lord said, "When the Comforter comes, whom I will send to you from the Father, the Spirit of reality, who proceeds from the Father, He will testify concerning Me." For the Spirit to testify concerning the Son means that He makes the Son real to us. The Father is embodied in the Son, and the Son is made real to us by the Spirit.

John 15, Romans 8, and Ephesians 3 are crucial portions of the Word concerning the dispensing function of the Triune God. The seed of this truth is in John 15, and the harvest of this truth is in Romans 8 and Ephesians 3. These portions not only give us the revelation of the Triune God but also show us how the Divine Trinity functions in a corporate way to dispense Himself into our being. This is not for doctrine but for our experience. All of us must see the dispensing function of the Triune God.

In the first section of John 14 the Lord unveiled to His disciples that He and the Father are one (vv. 9-11). He is in the Father, and the Father is in Him. His speaking was the Father's working. Then He went on to unveil that He and the Spirit are also one. This is from verse 16 through verse 20. So in John 14 you have these two main points: first, the Father is embodied in the Son, and second, the Son is realized as the Spirit.

John 14:23 says, "If anyone loves Me, he will keep My word, and My Father will love him, and We will come to him and make an abode with him." This is also the dispensing function of the Triune God. In John 14 there is the abode, and in chapter 15 there is the abiding. All these portions of the Word give us a clear picture that in the spiritual world there is the dispensing function of the Triune God into us, the tripartite men.

We also have to read Hebrews 8:10-11. Here it says that in the new covenant God has imparted His laws into our mind and inscribed them on our hearts. Therefore, we do not need anyone to teach us outwardly, because inwardly we have the subjective knowledge of God. We all can know God. The Greek word for *know* here is *oida,* which refers to the subjective knowledge of God. The dispensing function of the Triune God issues in the sense of life through the law of life. First John 2:27 goes on to speak of the anointing. The law of life and the anointing both issue in the sense of life and are both a part of the dispensing function of the Triune God.

I. GOD THE FATHER

A. Being the Source

First, we need to see that God the Father is the source. John 15:1b says that He is the husbandman, the source, and in Ephesians 3:14-16 the apostle Paul prays to the Father as the source.

B. Abiding in Us

The Father is also abiding in us. Ephesians 4:6 says that the Father is over all, through all, and in all. The Father dwells in us in the Son as the Spirit.

II. GOD THE SON

A. Being the Embodiment of the Father

In John 15:1a the Son said, "I am the true vine," and in John 14:11 He said that He is in the Father and the Father is in Him. Thus, the Son is the embodiment of the Father.

B. Abiding in Us and Making His Home in Our Hearts

In John 15:4a the Lord said, "Abide in Me and I in you." In Ephesians 3:17a Paul reveals that Christ is making His home in our hearts.

III. GOD THE SPIRIT

A. The Reality of the Son

The Son is the embodiment of the Father, and the Spirit is the reality of the Son. In our speaking to the saints, we need to develop the Lord's words in John 14:17-20, which reveal the Spirit as the reality of the Son.

B. Dwelling in Us

Romans 8:11 must be fully emphasized and developed to show the saints that in this one verse we can see that the Father is working, the Son is dispensing, and the Spirit is giving life. This verse shows us the functioning of the Father, the Son, and the Spirit to dispense life into our being, even into the circumference of our being. The body is the circumference of our being, and the spirit is the center of our being. The indwelling Triune God dispenses life to our whole being, and this dispensing reaches even to our circumference, our body.

IV. THE TRIUNE GOD— THE FATHER, THE SON, AND THE SPIRIT— DISPENSING HIMSELF INTO OUR BEING

In Ephesians 3:14-19 we can see that the Father hears the prayer and works to answer the prayer. Then the Spirit strengthens, and Christ makes His home to settle Himself in our hearts. The result is that we are filled unto all the fullness of God. Again, this is the functioning of the Triune God—the

Father, the Son, and the Spirit—to dispense Himself into our being.

V. THE DISPENSING FUNCTION OF THE TRIUNE GOD ISSUING IN THE SENSE OF LIFE

Actually, the sense of life comes from the dispensing function of the Triune God. Without the dispensing function of the Triune God, we would not have the sense of life. We would have only a deadened conscience. The sense of life is the issue of the Triune God functioning within us to dispense Himself as life into our whole being. We must show the saints how the sense of life is related to God's dispensing. Today we have the sense of life from the dispensing function of the Triune God in a living way, because the Father, the Son, and the Spirit cooperate together to function within us.

A. Through the Law of Life

The dispensing function of the Triune God issues in the sense of life through the law of life (Heb. 8:10-11). When the Triune God—the Father, the Son, and the Spirit—functions in us to dispense Himself into our being through the law of life, this issues in the sense of life.

B. By the Teaching of the Anointing

The issue of the sense of life by the dispensing function of the Triune God is by the teaching of the anointing (1 John 2:27). We have to build the saints up so that they may know all these terms. They should become very familiar with all these terms.

C. In Our Spirit Mingled with the Life-giving Spirit

Romans 8:16 says that the Spirit witnesses with our spirit. Then verse 14 says that as many as are led by the Spirit of God, these are sons of God. This shows that the dispensing function of the Triune God issuing in the sense of life is in our spirit mingled with the life-giving Spirit.

Thus, the sense of life is through the law of life, by the teaching of the anointing, and in our spirit, which is mingled with the life-giving Spirit. These three points are very crucial.

This is the real scientific study of the inner life. If we do not experience these things, they are hard to understand. We need to tell the saints that this needs experience. We should not merely exercise our mind to analyze these things. Without experience we cannot understand them. We have to prove the matters of life by our experience.

THE DIVINE LIFE DISPENSED INTO THE THREE PARTS OF MAN

Scripture Reading: Rom. 8:2a, 6, 9-11

OUTLINE

I. The divine life—Rom. 8:2a:
   A. The Spirit of life.
   B. In Christ Jesus.
II. Dispensed into our spirit—v. 10:
   A. Christ in you.
   B. The spirit being life.
III. Dispensed into our mind—v. 6b:
   A. The mind set on the spirit.
   B. The mind being life.
IV. Dispensed into our body—v. 11:
   A. Through God's indwelling Spirit.
   B. To give life to our mortal body.
V. The dispensing of the Triune God—vv. 9-10a:
   A. God.
   B. The Spirit of God.
   C. The Spirit of Christ.
   D. Christ.

Romans 8 reveals the divine life dispensed into the three parts of man. Verse 2a speaks of the law of the Spirit of life. Verse 6b says that the mind set on the spirit is life. Verse 10 says that if Christ is in us, the body is dead, but the spirit is life. Then verse 11 says that the Spirit of the One who raised Christ Jesus from the dead will give life to our mortal body through His Spirit who indwells us. Thus, verse 2 speaks of the divine life, verse 10 says that our spirit is life, verse 6 says that our mind can be life, and verse 11 says that even our body may be given life. Verse 8 speaks of God, verse 9 of the Spirit of God and the Spirit of Christ, and verse 10 of Christ. We need to read these verses to the saints to show them that the Triune God is dispensed into the three parts of man. While we are reading, it is always profitable to point out the crucial points in every verse.

I. THE DIVINE LIFE

A. The Spirit of Life

Romans 8:2 speaks of the Spirit of life. *The Spirit of life* is a phrase of apposition and actually means that the Spirit is life. In the Bible there are a number of phrases like this. *The Spirit of God* means that the Spirit is God; *the life of God* means that the life is God; *the Spirit of Christ* means that the Spirit is Christ; and *the love of God* means that love is God.

Of course, we know that if there is no Spirit of God, surely there is no life. Life is the Spirit. In Revelation 22:1 there is a picture of the river of water of life, and that river is the Spirit. This river flows out of the throne of God and of the Lamb. This shows how God in Christ as the Spirit flows Himself into His redeemed people to be their life and life supply. The river is the flow of life; it is life in motion.

This is like the current of electricity. Actually, the current itself is electricity. It is not something separate from electricity; it is electricity itself in motion. When electricity flows and is in motion, that is the current of electricity. The current of electricity can be compared to the Spirit of life. *The Spirit of life* means that the Spirit is life. The Spirit is life in motion, the Triune God in motion.

B. In Christ Jesus

This life is of the Spirit and is also in Christ Jesus. Romans 8:2 speaks of the Spirit of life freeing us in Christ Jesus. The phrase *in Christ Jesus* is profound. I believe that this phrase will need eternity for us to understand adequately. Today we understand a little. But when we enter into eternity, we will be freed from so many limitations, and then we will realize what it means to be in Christ Jesus.

In giving such a message, you have to define who Christ is and who Jesus is. The constituents of these two titles are profound. We have a life that is in Christ Jesus. The life is in such a One who is not only God and the Spirit but who is also Christ Jesus. Christ Jesus, this wonderful person, is constituted with many excellent elements. He is the One who has divinity and humanity, who has passed through so many processes, and who has accomplished so much. The life we are enjoying today is a life in such a realm and sphere. This realm and this sphere are an unlimited person, Christ Jesus.

In Romans 8:2 the Spirit of life frees us in Christ Jesus, not in Jesus Christ. The life is in Christ, and it traces back from Christ to Jesus. We need to let the saints know that *in Christ Jesus* is not an empty term. If it were an empty term, Paul would not use it. Surely this means a lot. We must tell the saints that the very divine life today is not only of the Spirit but is also in such a marvelous, unlimited person as its realm, its sphere.

II. DISPENSED INTO OUR SPIRIT

Such a divine life is first dispensed into our spirit. Romans 8:10 says that since Christ is in us, our spirit is life. This is because Christ Himself is this life, and this life is in our spirit. Therefore, our spirit is life. This is a very strong point. Verse 10 does not say that since Christ is in us, the life is in us. Instead, it says that our spirit is life. Today our regenerated spirit is life.

The contrast presented in verse 10 is very interesting. It says that if Christ is in you, your body is dead. It does not say that your body is death. The opposite of being dead is being living. Based upon this, it would seem that verse 10 should say that our body is dead and our spirit is living. But here Paul makes the contrast different. He says that our body is dead and our spirit is life. Since Christ is in our spirit, our spirit is not only living but also life.

We may read Romans 8:10, which says that our spirit is life, yet understand that either life is in our spirit or that our spirit is living. We read this verse in one way, but we realize it subconsciously in another way, in a natural way. We do not realize that our fallen spirit, after being regenerated with Christ, becomes life. It is not only living and does not only have life; it is life itself.

Paul did not use all these words and phrases in a light way. He wrote Romans just as an attorney would write a legal document. In Romans 8 every word, every phrase, every clause, and every sentence should have been thoroughly considered by Paul. Paul was very careful about the experience of life and about the truth. All the things in Romans 8 are greatly involved with life and truth. Paul says that since Christ is in us, our spirit is life. Now that we have been saved, we have a part of our being that is life itself.

A. Christ in You

We have to stress strongly that Christ is in us. Life is not good behavior. Life is Christ. Any kind of virtue is not life, regardless of how high or how excellent that virtue is. Life is a person. Life is Christ Himself, and Christ is in us. We have to stress this strongly. We can never overly stress this one thing— "Christ in you." We are short of utterance to stress this one thing. In the whole universe nothing is greater than Christ being in us. Christ being in us is the greatest wonder, the wonder of wonders, in the whole universe. We need to impress the saints with who Christ is. He is both God and man, having both divinity and humanity. We have to stress again and again all the wonderful riches of Christ. Such a One is now in us.

We should not take Romans 8 for granted. It is not a small thing that Romans 8 was written and that this chapter is in the Bible. Without Romans 8, what would we do as Christians?

We must stress the wonder of Christ being in us to impress ourselves and impress the saints.

B. The Spirit Being Life

Because Christ is in us, our spirit is life. Regeneration is a mingling work to mingle Christ with our spirit. Today Christ is life, and our spirit is also life. This is because our spirit has been made one with Christ, who is life. First Corinthians 6:17 says, "He who is joined to the Lord is one spirit." Surely this one spirit comprises both Christ and our spirit, so both Christ and our spirit today are life. This is why we need to exercise our spirit. If we exercise our spirit, life will be infused into people because our spirit is life. If we exercise our spirit to minister to others, then our spirit will reach others as life.

III. DISPENSED INTO OUR MIND

Romans 8:6 says that the mind set on the spirit is life. Not only our spirit is life; even our mind can be life. But this mind must be set on the spirit. This means that this mind must be flooded, saturated, and infused with the spirit to become the mind of the spirit. Eventually, the spirit becomes the spirit of our mind. This is mentioned in Ephesians 4:23. Because our mind is set on the spirit, our spirit saturates our mind and makes our mind a mind of the spirit. Eventually, our spirit becomes the spirit of our mind. The renewing is by this spirit that saturates our mind. We always have to tell the saints that this spirit is the mingled spirit. It is our spirit mingled with Christ as the life-giving Spirit.

Because our mind is one with our spirit, connected, joined, saturated, and infused with our spirit, our mind is also life. Such a mind can function to minister life to others. By our natural mind we cannot minister life to others. This mind is not life. But when our mind is joined to our spirit and is saturated with our spirit that is life, our mind at this time also becomes life.

A. The Mind Set on the Spirit

For this point we have to say that the mind set on the spirit means that the mind is joined to the spirit and is relying on the spirit. The spirit can be likened to the husband, and the mind to the wife. The mind as the wife should always rely upon the spirit as the husband. The mind should always depend upon the spirit. Just as the wife and the husband are really one couple, the mind and the spirit are really one unit. They are no longer separated.

Romans 1:28 speaks of the fallen mind as a disapproved mind, a reprobate mind. A reprobate mind is one that rejects God and that is rejected by God. It is a mind that disapproves of knowing God and is also disapproved by God. That was our original mind in its fallen state.

Romans 7 shows us that a saved person seeking to serve God uses his natural mind to keep the law and is defeated (vv. 23, 25). In chapter 7 the mind is no longer reprobate, but it is still independent. It is living like a widow, having the heart and desire to do things but without a husband to rely on. The mind in chapter 1 is a reprobate one, but the mind in chapter 7 is a seeking one, seeking after God and trying to please God but not relying on the spirit.

Romans 8 also mentions the mind, but the mind here is set on the spirit. Now the mind as the widow has married a new husband. It is not just a seeking mind but a married mind, a mind married to the spirit. Such a mind becomes one with the spirit, and because of this, such a mind also becomes life. The fourth place that talks about the mind in Romans is 12:2, which speaks of the renewing of the mind. Such a relying mind must be renewed. Thus, in Romans we see the reprobate mind, the seeking mind, the relying mind, and eventually the renewed mind. In order for us to have a renewed mind, we need the mind relying on, depending on, the spirit.

B. The Mind Being Life

First our spirit becomes life, and then our mind becomes life. This means that the divine life has spread from within our spirit into our soul to saturate our mind. Here we need to tell the saints that our mind actually represents our soul. It is not too much to say that the mind here is our soul. The mind here is the soul because it is the main part of our soul. When our mind is really married to our spirit, set on our spirit, relying on our spirit to be one with our spirit, such a mind becomes life.

IV. DISPENSED INTO OUR BODY

Romans 8:11 says that the Spirit of the very God who raised Christ Jesus from the dead gives life to our mortal body, our dying body, through the Spirit who indwells us. The word *mortal* in this verse implies not only the thought of death but also the thought of weakness. A mortal body is a weakened body, a dying body. Romans 7 calls our fallen body the body of this death (v. 24). Even such a weakened, dying, mortal body, a body of death, can be given life.

Thus far, we can see that the divine life mentioned in Romans 8:2 is imparted, or dispensed, into our spirit in verse 10 and spreads into our mind in verse 6. Then it is dispensed into our mortal body in verse 11. Thus, the divine life is dispensed into all three parts of our being.

A. Through God's Indwelling Spirit

This dispensing of life into our mortal body is through the indwelling Spirit. Without the Spirit indwelling us, life cannot be dispensed from the center of our being to the circumference of our being. Our spirit is our center, and our body is our circumference. So the divine life first is dispensed into the center, and from the center it spreads to the circumference. Then our body is enlivened through the indwelling Spirit.

B. To Give Life to Our Mortal Body

We have covered this already, but when we give this lesson, we need to dwell upon this point. Very few Christians realize that the divine life can even be dispensed into our body. We should give the saints some illustrations of this. Sometimes after work in the evening, we are worn out and weakened and do not think we can attend the meeting. But if we would exercise our spirit to pray and contact the Lord, this will allow the indwelling Spirit to move in us. Spontaneously, the divine life will be dispensed into our weakened body, and our weakened body will be vitalized. Then we will have the physical strength to go to the meeting. This is a proof that life can be dispensed into our weakened body.

Brother Watchman Nee practiced this. He had a very troublesome heart that was always weakening his body. Many times while he was speaking, the trouble came. He no doubt at that juncture exercised his spirit to let the indwelling Spirit vitalize, or enliven, his weakened body so that his body did not frustrate or delay his ministry. He surely experienced the divine life being dispensed from his spirit into his weakened body. We can also give testimonies of our own experiences in this matter. Our weakened, dying, or sick body can be vitalized by the divine life through the indwelling Spirit.

V. THE DISPENSING OF THE TRIUNE GOD

The final thing we need to stress in this message is the dispensing of the Triune God. We need to say repeatedly that in Romans 8 there is the dispensing of the Triune God. In verses 8 through 10 four titles are interchangeably used: *God, the Spirit of God, the Spirit of Christ,* and *Christ.* God is the Spirit of God, the Spirit of God is the Spirit of Christ, and the Spirit of Christ is Christ Himself. Without God being the Spirit, God could not reach us. In order for electricity to reach a building, it has to become a current. The current of electricity is the reaching of electricity. In like manner, the Spirit of God is God's reaching us.

Also, for God to reach us and for the Spirit of God to reach us, He has to be the Spirit of Christ. This is because with Christ there are two main things: humanity and redemption. The Spirit of God has to be the Spirit of Christ because there is the need of humanity and redemption. His incarnation gave Him humanity, and His crucifixion accomplished redemption. Through humanity and redemption the Spirit became the reaching Spirit. The Spirit of God is now the Spirit of Christ with humanity and redemption for reaching us.

We should not read all these verses and take them for granted. We must say, "Lord, open our eyes. We must see something." Romans 8 shows us the dispensing of the Triune God as the divine life into the three parts of man. Eventually, verse 11 says that the God who raised Christ Jesus from the dead gives life to our mortal body through the indwelling Spirit. This verse gives us a full picture of the Triune God dispensing life into our being from the center to the circumference. This dispensing comes from these four titles: *God, the Spirit of God, the Spirit of Christ,* and *Christ.*

Romans 8:9-11 gives us a full picture of the dispensing of the Triune God for the purpose of imparting Himself into us as the divine life. First, He dispenses Himself into our spirit; then He spreads to our mind; and finally, He reaches our mortal body. Then our whole being is saturated with the divine life. Actually, this divine life is the dispensing Triune God Himself. We must be very clear about what life is. In the previous lesson we saw the dispensing function of the Triune God issuing in the sense of life. In this lesson we have seen the divine life dispensed into the three parts of man.

THE SENSE OF THE SPIRIT AND KNOWING THE SPIRIT

(1)

Scripture Reading: Rom. 8:2, 6

OUTLINE

I. Four things:
   A. Life—Rom. 8:2a:
      1. The Spirit of life.
      2. The Spirit containing life and belonging to life.
      3. The Spirit being the source of life, and life being the issue of the Spirit—v. 6b.
   B. Law—v. 2a:
      1. The Spirit not only belonging to life but also having its law.
      2. Life being the content and issue of the Spirit; the law of life being the function and action of the Spirit.
      3. By contacting life we touch the Spirit; by sensing the law we also sense the Spirit.
   C. Peace—v. 6b:
      1. Peace being also the issue of the spirit.
      2. Touching the spirit, we do not only touch life but also peace.
   D. Death—v. 6a:
      1. Death being the issue of the flesh.
      2. The sense of death causing us to know the things of the flesh, thus unveiling the spirit from the negative side.

In this lesson we want to see the sense of the spirit and knowing the spirit. The *spirit* here refers to our spirit indwelt by the Spirit of God, so it is the mingled spirit. We again want to refer to Romans 8:2 and 6. Verse 2 speaks of the law of the Spirit of life, and verse 6 says that the mind set on the flesh is death, but the mind set on the spirit is life and peace.

In these two verses there are four main things that we need to pay attention to. In verse 2 we have to pay attention to the words *life* and *law*. Then in verse 6 we have to pay attention to the words *peace* and *death*. In order to know the sense of the spirit, we must know these four things: law, life, peace, and death. Actually, the sense of the spirit is realized through these four things.

I. FOUR THINGS:

A. Life

1. The Spirit of Life

We saw in the previous lesson that *the Spirit of life* actually means that the Spirit is life. What is life? Life is the Spirit, so the Spirit is called the Spirit of life. This life is not our physical life or our soulish life but the very divine life, the life of God, the eternal, uncreated life, which has been imparted into our spirit to be our life.

Within every genuine Christian there are three lives: the physical life, the psychological life, and the spiritual, divine life. Three different Greek words are used for these three lives: *bios*—the physical life, *psuche*—the soulish life, and *zoe*—the spiritual life. What we are talking about in these lessons is zoe, which is the divine life, the eternal life, the life of God, becoming our spiritual life. This life is the Spirit of God Himself.

2. The Spirit Containing Life and Belonging to Life

We have to stress here that the life we are talking about is the content of the Spirit, and the Spirit belongs to this life. Many Christians consider eternal life as a kind of eternal, blessed situation or environment. To them it is a place where they will go to enjoy good things for eternity. This is absolutely wrong.

We must stress that the divine life is a person, who is the very Spirit Himself.

When many refer to life, they do not know that there are three different Greek words for *life*. They think that *life* refers to our life. Among many Christians the matter of life is very ambiguous. The Gospel of John says that when we believe into the Lord Jesus, we receive eternal life (3:16, 36a). This life is a person, and this person today is the Spirit. Life is the content of this person, and this person belongs to this life.

3. The Spirit Being the Source of Life, and Life Being the Issue of the Spirit

Here we need to use Romans 8:6b, which says that the mind set on the spirit is life and peace. This indicates that the Spirit is the source of life, and life is the issue of the Spirit. In other words, this life is altogether one with the Spirit. This life cannot be separated from the Spirit. The Spirit is the container and this life is the content; the Spirit is the source and this life is the issue.

B. Law

1. The Spirit Not Only Belonging to Life but Also Having Its Law

Romans 8:2a speaks of "the law of the Spirit of life." This shows that the Spirit not only belongs to life but also has the life law as the law of life.

2. Life Being the Content and Issue of the Spirit; the Law of Life Being the Function and Action of the Spirit

Life is the content and issue of the Spirit, whereas the law of life is the function and action of the Spirit. When the Spirit functions, this function is the law. When the Spirit acts, this action is the law.

3. By Contacting Life We Touch the Spirit; by Sensing the Law We Also Sense the Spirit

We can realize the Spirit by contacting life and by sensing

the law. By this we can see that the phrase *the law of the Spirit of life* is somewhat complicated. The law, the Spirit, and life are wrapped up together as one unit. Life is the content and issue of the Spirit, and the law of life is the function and action of the Spirit. Thus, when we contact life, we touch the Spirit, and when we sense the law, we sense the Spirit. This is because life and the law of life are both one with the Spirit.

C. Peace

1. Peace Being Also the Issue of the Spirit

Romans 8:6b says that the mind set on the spirit is life and peace. In addition to life, peace is also the issue of the spirit.

2. Touching the Spirit, We Do Not Only Touch Life but Also Peace

We should not forget that this is a continuation of our fellowship in Lesson 11 on the sense of life. We have to point out that the feeling of peace is the inner feeling of ease, comfort, harmony, rest, joy, and liberty. When we touch the spirit, we touch life, and at the same time we also touch peace.

D. Death

1. Death Being the Issue of the Flesh

Romans 8:6a says that the mind set on the flesh is death. Life is the issue of the spirit; death is the issue of the flesh. Death comes out of the flesh.

2. The Sense of Death Causing Us to Know the Things of the Flesh, Thus Unveiling the Spirit from the Negative Side

The sense of death causes us to know the things of the flesh. We know death because we have the feeling, the consciousness, of death. The inner feelings of dissatisfaction, emptiness, oldness, dryness, darkness, and depression are aspects of the sense of death versus the sense of life. Also, the inner feelings of strife, discord, discomfort, restlessness, pain, bondage, and grief are aspects of the sense of death versus the sense of peace.

By these four things—life, the law of life, peace, and death—

we can realize the sense of the spirit. Then by the sense of the spirit, we can know the spirit. The spirit may be likened to electricity. No one can see it. It can only be realized by its issue. We know that electricity is present in a room because of the lights in a room. The spirit is the same. No one can see the spirit, but with the spirit there are many issues, such as the issue of life, the issue of the law of life, the issue of peace, and the issue of death. Death is a negative issue, the issue on the negative side, to point us to something on the positive side. By the consciousness of life, the consciousness of the law of life, the consciousness of peace, and the consciousness of death, we can sense the spirit. We can know the spirit by the sense of the spirit.

THE SENSE OF THE SPIRIT AND KNOWING THE SPIRIT

(2)

Scripture Reading: Rom. 8:2, 6

OUTLINE

II. Consciousness:
  A. Of life:
    1. The higher the life, the richer its consciousness.
    2. The divine life being the highest life with the richest consciousness.
    3. This life within us causing us to be full of spiritual consciousness, enabling us to sense the spirit and the things of the spirit.
  B. Of the law of life:
    1. The law of a conscious life belonging to the realm of consciousness.
    2. The law of the Spirit of life being full of consciousness.
  C. Of peace:
    1. The peace within us being entirely a matter of consciousness.
    2. The consciousness of peace enabling us to know that we are in the spirit.
  D. Of death:
    1. Death causing us to lose consciousness.
    2. Death also causing us to have the sense of death.
III. Knowing the spirit by the sense of the spirit:
  A. By the sense of life:

    1. The divine life being contained in the Holy Spirit.

    2. The Holy Spirit mingling Himself with our spirit.

    3. The divine life becoming the life of the Holy Spirit and of our spirit.

    4. This divine life in the Holy Spirit through our spirit giving us the senses of life.

    5. By such a sense of life we know the spirit.

B. By the sense of the law of life:

    1. The law of life being the natural function of the divine life.

    2. The functioning of the law of life.

    3. The law of life giving us the natural sense on the positive side and the unnatural sense on the negative side.

    4. The natural sense versus the unnatural sense of the law of life.

C. By the sense of peace:

    1. The life of the Holy Spirit in our spirit being God Himself.

    2. Our spirit with the divine life contained in the Holy Spirit being the new man.

    3. God as our life versus our self.

    4. The new man versus our old man.

    5. The sense of peace being the issue of walking and living by the divine life.

    6. By such a sense of peace we know that we are living in the spirit.

D. By the sense of death:

    1. Death being the issue of our flesh, including our old man.

    2. Death being the opposite of both life and peace.

    3. The negative senses of death.

    4. By such negative senses, we know that we are not in the spirit.

In this lesson we want to continue our fellowship on the sense of the spirit and knowing the spirit. In the previous lesson we saw four things related to the sense of the spirit: life, the law of life, peace, and death. Now we want to talk about the consciousness of these four things and about how to know the spirit by the sense of the spirit.

II. CONSCIOUSNESS

A. Of Life

1. The Higher the Life, the Richer Its Consciousness

Life has its own consciousness; it has its own sense. The higher the life is, the richer its consciousness is. The plant life is the lowest life, so it has nearly no consciousness. Then in the animal life there are different levels of consciousness. The consciousness of life on different levels differs according to the standard of life. Our human life is higher than the animal life, so the human life has a richer consciousness. The divine life, of course, has the richest consciousness.

2. The Divine Life Being the Highest Life with the Richest Consciousness

Among all the different lives, the divine life is the highest, so it has the richest consciousness.

3. This Life within Us Causing Us to Be Full of Spiritual Consciousness, Enabling Us to Sense the Spirit and the Things of the Spirit

The divine life in us causes us to be full of spiritual consciousness. The more we are filled with this divine life, the more we are filled with spiritual consciousness. This enables us to sense the spirit and also to sense the things of the spirit. This is the consciousness of life.

B. Of the Law of Life

1. The Law of a Conscious Life Belonging to the Realm of Consciousness

The law of life is not a law of something that has no consciousness, but it is the law of a conscious life. Thus, it belongs to the realm of consciousness.

2. The Law of the Spirit of Life
Being Full of Consciousness

The law of the Spirit of life is something in the sphere of consciousness and is full of consciousness.

C. Of Peace

1. The Peace within Us
Being Entirely a Matter of Consciousness

The peace within us is not the peace in the environment. This is the peace within our being. It is entirely a matter of consciousness. We know that there is peace within us by the inner consciousness.

2. The Consciousness of Peace
Enabling Us to Know That We Are in the Spirit

This consciousness of peace enables us to know that we are in the spirit. If we do not have peace, this indicates that we are not in the spirit. If we have peace, if we sense peace within us, this tells us that we are in the spirit.

D. Of Death

1. Death Causing Us to Lose Consciousness

Death first causes us to lose consciousness, because a dead person does not have any kind of consciousness.

2. Death Also Causing Us
to Have the Sense of Death

On the one hand, death causes us to lose our consciousness, to become numb. On the other hand, death also causes us to have the sense of death. The sense of death is the sense of uneasiness, discomfort, depression, oppression, darkness, and emptiness. When we sense these things within us, this indicates that death is within us.

III. KNOWING THE SPIRIT
BY THE SENSE OF THE SPIRIT

After we realize the consciousness of life, the law of life, peace, and death, we can know the spirit by the sense of the spirit.

A. By the Sense of Life

1. The Divine Life
Being Contained in the Holy Spirit

The divine life is contained in the Holy Spirit. According to Romans 8:2, the Holy Spirit is the Spirit of life.

2. The Holy Spirit Mingling
Himself with Our Spirit

When we were regenerated, the Holy Spirit mingled Himself with our spirit (v. 16; 1 Cor. 6:17).

3. The Divine Life Becoming
the Life of the Holy Spirit and of Our Spirit

The divine life is mentioned in Romans 8:2, which refers to the law of the Spirit of life. Eventually, the divine life becomes the life not only of the Holy Spirit but also of our spirit, because now the Holy Spirit in whom the divine life is contained mingles Himself with our spirit. These two spirits have become one, so the divine life is the life of both of the two spirits, the Holy Spirit and our spirit.

4. This Divine Life in the Holy Spirit
through Our Spirit Giving Us the Senses of Life

We can know the spirit by the inner sense of the spirit. The divine life in the Holy Spirit through our spirit gives us the sense of freshness, liveliness, strengthening, brightness, holiness, reality, satisfaction, etc.

5. By Such a Sense of Life We Know the Spirit

By the sense of life, we can know the spirit. When we sense all the above items deep within, that is the sense of life, and this sense proves that we are walking according to the spirit (v. 4).

B. By the Sense of the Law of Life

1. The Law of Life Being the Natural Function
of the Divine Life

We can also know the spirit by the sense of the law of life.

The law of life is the natural function of the divine life according to its divine nature. This means that the law of life functions according to the divine nature of the divine life.

2. The Functioning of the Law of Life

The law of life functions to approve and accept things corresponding with the divine nature, and it opposes and rejects things not corresponding with God's nature.

3. The Law of Life Giving Us the Natural Sense on the Positive Side and the Unnatural Sense on the Negative Side

The law of life always gives us some sense. Sometimes the sense is natural, on the positive side. This means that we are in the spirit. Sometimes the sense is unnatural, on the negative side. This means that we are not in the spirit.

4. The Natural Sense versus the Unnatural Sense of the Law of Life

By the natural sense of the law of life, we know that we are living in our spirit; by the unnatural sense of the law of life, we know that we are out of the spirit. These two senses are versus each other.

C. By the Sense of Peace

1. The Life of the Holy Spirit in Our Spirit Being God Himself

The life of the Holy Spirit is the life of God, and this life in our spirit is God Himself. The phrase *the life of God* (Eph. 4:18) means that the life is God.

2. Our Spirit with the Divine Life Contained in the Holy Spirit Being the New Man

The life in our spirit is God Himself, and our spirit with the divine life contained in the Holy Spirit is the new man.

3. God as Our life versus Our Self

God as our life is versus our self.

4. The New Man versus Our Old Man

Furthermore, the new man is versus our old man.

5. The Sense of Peace Being the Issue of Walking and Living by the Divine Life

When we walk and live by the divine life in our new man, we have the sense of peace, feeling natural, restful, comfortable, and at ease.

6. By Such a Sense of Peace We Know That We Are Living in the Spirit

When we have the inner sense of peace with the feeling of comfort, harmony, rest, joy, and liberty, we know that we are living in the spirit.

D. By the Sense of Death

1. Death Being the Issue of Our Flesh, including Our Old Man

Romans 8:6 says, "The mind set on the flesh is death." The flesh includes our old man. Death is the issue of our flesh, including our old man.

2. Death Being the Opposite of Both Life and Peace

Romans 8:6 shows us that death is the opposite of both life and peace. The mind set on the flesh is death, but the mind set on the spirit is life and peace.

3. The Negative Senses of Death

Death gives us the senses of oldness, dryness, weakness, emptiness, depression, desolation, darkness, dullness, uneasiness, insecurity, discomfort, unnaturalness, sadness, conflict, etc.

4. By Such Negative Senses, We Know That We Are Not in the Spirit

When we have such negative senses, we are sensing death. By such negative senses, we know that we are not in the spirit.

THE HUMAN SPIRIT

Scripture Reading: Gen. 2:7; Prov. 20:27; Zech. 12:1b; Rom. 9:1; John 4:24; Rom. 1:9; Luke 1:47; Rom. 8:16; Ezek. 36:26; 2 Tim. 4:22a; John 3:6b; 1 Cor. 6:17; Eph. 2:22b; Gal. 5:16, 25b; Rom. 8:4b; Rev. 1:10a

OUTLINE

I. The creation of the human spirit:
   A. By Jehovah God breathing the breath of life into man—Gen. 2:7.
   B. The breath of life becoming man's spirit—Prov. 20:27.
II. The importance of the human spirit—ranked with the heavens and the earth—Zech. 12:1b.
III. The three parts of the human spirit:
   A. The conscience—Rom. 9:1, cf. 8:16; 1 Cor. 5:3; Psa. 51:10; 34:18; Deut. 2:30.
   B. Fellowship—John 4:24; Rom. 1:9; 7:6; Eph. 6:18; Luke 1:47; Rom. 8:16; 1 Cor. 6:17.
   C. Intuition—2:11; Mark 2:8; 8:12; John 11:33.
IV. The function of the human spirit:
   A. To contact God—4:24.
   B. To receive God—Ezek. 36:26.
   C. To contain God—2 Tim. 4:22a.
V. Being deadened—Eph. 2:1, 5a.
VI. Being regenerated—John 3:6b:
   A. By God the Spirit.
   B. With God's life—1:13b.
VII. To be one spirit with the Lord—1 Cor. 6:17; Rom. 8:16.
VIII. To be the dwelling place of God—Eph. 2:22b.
IX. Walking by the spirit and according to the spirit—Gal. 5:16, 25b; Rom. 8:4b; Rev. 1:10a.

All the saints need some basic knowledge of the human spirit. This is a great topic, but it is good to have this basic lesson to give the new ones and young ones a general knowledge of this important yet greatly missed point in the Bible. In these lessons as well as in the other lessons, I am presenting some basic points to you for your further study and development.

I. THE CREATION OF THE HUMAN SPIRIT

If we are going to see the human spirit, we have to see its source, its creation.

A. By Jehovah God Breathing the Breath of Life into Man

Genesis 1:1 says that in the beginning God created the heavens and the earth. In this verse the title for God is *Elohim*. It is not until chapter 2 that *Jehovah* is used as a title for God. Genesis 2:7 says that Jehovah God breathed the breath of life into man. God as *Elohim* was mainly related to the creation of the universe. But God in His title of *Jehovah* is mainly related to His relationship with man. *Jehovah* is a title for God in His contact with man. In Genesis 2 this title is used especially when it mentions that God created a spirit in man by breathing the breath of life into man.

Job 33:4 says, "The Spirit of God has made me, / And the breath of the Almighty has enlivened me." The breath of life here is called the breath of the Almighty. We cannot say, however, that this breath is the life of God or the Spirit of God. The most we can say according to the Bible is that it is the breath of life, the breath of the Almighty. Thus, it is very close to God's life and very close to God's Spirit.

Some Bible teachers wrongly consider that this breath of life is something directly of God's life and of God's Spirit. It might be that they think that this is the same breathing that the Lord Jesus did in John 20:22 when He breathed the Holy Spirit into the disciples. But the following chapters and books of the Bible clearly reveal that although man at that time had the breath of life, he did not have God's life or God's Spirit. What was breathed into man was just the breath of life, but we must be clear that it is very close to the life of God and very close to the Spirit of God.

The creation of man's spirit was not like the creation of his body. Man's body was formed from the dust of the ground, having nothing to do with God's life or with God's Spirit. It was formed of physical, material dust. But the material for the creation of man's spirit, the breath of life, was very close to the life of God and to the Spirit of God. This indicates strongly that this organ of the human being is not for material things or for psychological things. This organ is for the divine life and the divine Spirit.

The human life with the human spirit is very similar to God's life and God's Spirit because two lives must be very similar for them to be grafted into one. When man's body was formed from the dust, there was no life in man. When the breath of life was breathed into that form of dust, man became a living soul. Man became something with life, and that life came from God's breath of life. Job 33:4 says that the breath of the Almighty enlivened man. This is similar to Genesis 2:7. This shows us that man was created by God with a life and a spirit, which are very close to the divine life and the divine Spirit. Man is similar to God in this way so that he can be grafted into God in the divine life.

B. The Breath of Life Becoming Man's Spirit

Proverbs 20:27 says, "The spirit of man is the lamp of Jehovah." Generally speaking, the word in Hebrew for *spirit* is *ruach,* but the Hebrew word for *spirit* here is *neshamah. Neshamah* is the same word used in Genesis 2:7 for *breath.* In Proverbs 20:27 it is translated "spirit." By this we can see that the breath of life breathed into man by God at man's creation was the spirit of man. The spirit of man is something within us that is very close to God's life and God's Spirit. This indicates that the spirit of man was created for the purpose of receiving and containing the life of God and the Spirit of God. Eventually, 1 Corinthians 6:17 says, "He who is joined to the Lord is one spirit." Our spirit can become one spirit with the Lord because it was created with the breath of life, which is very close to God's life and God's Spirit.

II. THE IMPORTANCE OF THE HUMAN SPIRIT—
RANKED WITH THE HEAVENS AND THE EARTH

Zechariah 12:1 says that Jehovah stretches forth the heavens, lays the foundations of the earth, and forms the spirit of man within him. No one can deny that these three items—the heavens, the earth, and the spirit of man—are crucial in God's creation to fulfill His purpose. The heavens were created for the earth, the earth was created for man, and man was created for God.

Zechariah does not refer to "man" but to "the spirit of man." This is because the spirit of man is the very organ that can take in God to enjoy God's life and God's Spirit and be one with God's Spirit. This is why man's spirit has become so crucial and important, even to the extent that it is ranked with the heavens and the earth. The philosophy of man does not rank anything of man with the heavens and the earth, but Zechariah ranks man's spirit with them. This shows how important the human spirit is.

We have to point this out to the saints. We need to give a training lesson in which we point out that our human spirit was created with a material that is very close to God's life and Spirit. We also need to point out that our spirit is so important that it is ranked with the heavens and the earth.

III. THE THREE PARTS OF THE HUMAN SPIRIT

A. The Conscience

It is not easy to pick up a verse or verses that directly show that the conscience is a part of the spirit. We have to compare Romans 9:1 with 8:16. Romans 9:1 says that our conscience bears witness with us in the Holy Spirit, whereas 8:16 says that the Spirit witnesses with our spirit. These two verses strongly prove that our conscience is a part of our spirit. In 1 Corinthians 5:3 Paul judged a sinful one in his spirit. To judge is to condemn sin, and that is mostly the function of the conscience. Psalm 51:10 speaks of "a right spirit within me" (KJV). This is a spirit that is right. Knowing right from wrong is related to the conscience, so this verse shows that the conscience is in the spirit. Other verses we can use to show the function of the conscience as a part of the spirit are Psalm 34:18 and

Deuteronomy 2:30. For verses related to the parts of the human spirit, we need to read chapter 6 of *The Economy of God.*

B. Fellowship

Another part, or function, of our human spirit is the fellowship. John 4:24 says, "God is Spirit, and those who worship Him must worship in spirit." This worship is a kind of fellowship, a kind of contact. In Romans 1:9 Paul says that he served God in his spirit and in 7:6 that he served God in newness of spirit. Ephesians 6:18 says to pray at every time in spirit. To pray also is to fellowship with God. In Luke 1:47 Mary said that her spirit exulted, rejoiced, in God. That surely is a kind of fellowship. Romans 8:16 and 1 Corinthians 6:17 show that our spirit is one spirit with the Lord. That oneness is also a kind of fellowship. All the above verses can be used to prove that in our spirit there is something called fellowship.

C. Intuition

The intuition is also a part of man's spirit. First Corinthians 2:11 says that the spirit of man knows the things of man. The spirit can know what the soul cannot know. Verses 14 and 15 say that a soulish man cannot receive the things of God but that the spiritual man can. The direct sense in our spirit regardless of reason or circumstances is the intuition. The intuition is a direct sense of God and a direct knowledge from God. Mark 2:8 and 8:12 and John 11:33 are other verses showing that the intuition is a part of the human spirit. These verses show that in the human spirit, there is a direct sense of discernment to know God and the spiritual things. This direct sense is the intuition.

Thus, we can see that the conscience functions to discern right from wrong, the fellowship functions to contact God, and the intuition functions to know God and to know God's will, God's intention.

IV. THE FUNCTION OF THE HUMAN SPIRIT

A. To Contact God

John 4:24 shows that the function of the human spirit is to contact God.

B. To Receive God

Ezekiel 36:26 says that God gives us a new heart and a new spirit. The new heart is for loving God and seeking after God, whereas the new spirit is for receiving God. The heart is the loving and seeking organ, and the spirit is the receiving organ. We all have a heart to love certain things. A person may love tea, but if he does not have a stomach, he has no organ to receive the tea. This shows that we need a new heart to love God and a new spirit to receive God.

C. To Contain God

Second Timothy 4:22 says, "The Lord be with your spirit." Our spirit is the place where God stays within us, so our spirit is a container of God.

V. BEING DEADENED

Our human spirit was deadened by the fall. Ephesians 2 says that we were dead in our offenses and sins (vv. 1, 5a). This death was not in man's physical body or in his psychological being. Due to the fall, man was deadened in his spirit. This means that his spirit lost its function. The deadness of man's spirit, which pervaded his entire being, caused him to lose the function that enabled him to contact God.

VI. BEING REGENERATED

A. By God the Spirit

John 3:6b says, "That which is born of the Spirit is spirit." Our regeneration was carried out in the human spirit by God the Spirit.

B. With God's Life

We were regenerated with God's life—the uncreated, eternal life. Thus, to be regenerated is to have the divine, eternal life (in addition to the human, natural life) as the new source and new element of a new person. John 1:13b says that we were begotten of God. To be regenerated is to be begotten of God with the Father's life, the divine life.

VII. TO BE ONE SPIRIT WITH THE LORD

The human spirit was created for a purpose. God created this organ of man so that man could be one spirit with the Lord. First Corinthians 6:17 says, "He who is joined to the Lord is one spirit." This may be the most important verse in the whole Bible. Romans 8:16 says that the divine Spirit witnesses with our human spirit. Now these two spirits are one.

VIII. TO BE THE DWELLING PLACE OF GOD

Ephesians 2:22 says that we are being built together into a dwelling place of God in spirit. The Holy Spirit is the Dweller, not the dwelling place. Our spirit is the dwelling place. This proves that our spirit was made to contain God within us.

IX. WALKING BY THE SPIRIT
AND ACCORDING TO THE SPIRIT

Galatians 5:16 and 25b charge us to walk by the Spirit, and Romans 8:4 says that we need to walk according to the spirit. In Revelation 1:10 the apostle John said that he was in spirit on the Lord's Day. This shows that we need to have a life in the spirit. John was a man in the spirit. This means that we need to live in the spirit.

All the new ones and young ones among us need to have a strong understanding of the human spirit. The truth concerning the human spirit is the basic element for many teachings in the Lord's recovery. If the saints have not been brought into an adequate knowledge of the human spirit, they will be somewhat weak in the understanding of all the spiritual things.

THE EXERCISE OF OUR SPIRIT

Scripture Reading: Prov. 20:27; 1 Pet. 3:4; Eph. 3:16; Ezra 1:1, 5; Rom. 12:11; Acts 18:25; Eph. 6:18; John 4:24; Luke 1:46-47; 1 Cor. 14:32; 2:11a; Mark 2:8a; Acts 19:21a; 1 Cor. 5:3-5a; Rev. 1:10

OUTLINE

I. Our spirit being the lamp of the Lord, searching all our inward parts—Prov. 20:27.

II. Our spirit being the hidden man of the heart—1 Pet. 3:4.

III. Our regenerated spirit being our inner man—Eph. 3:16.

IV. Our spirit needing to be stirred up—Ezra 1:1, 5; cf. Exo. 35:21.

V. Our spirit needing to be burning—Rom. 12:11; Acts 18:25.

VI. Our spirit indwelt by the Holy Spirit needing to be the faculty of our prayer—Eph. 6:18.

VII. Our spirit needing to be the means of our worship—John 4:24.

VIII. Our spirit needing to take the lead in enjoying the Lord—Luke 1:46-47.

IX. Our spirit needing to take the initiative in spiritual ministry—1 Cor. 14:32.

X. Our spirit knowing the things of man—2:11a.

XI. Perceiving things in our spirit—Mark 2:8a.

XII. Purposing in our spirit—Acts 19:21a.

XIII. Judging a person in our spirit—1 Cor. 5:3-5a.

XIV. Being a person in our spirit—Rev. 1:10.

XV. Exercising our spirit by doing the abovementioned things.

Now that we have seen something concerning the human spirit, we need to go on to see the exercise of our spirit.

I. OUR SPIRIT BEING THE LAMP OF THE LORD, SEARCHING ALL OUR INWARD PARTS

Proverbs 20:27 says that our spirit is the lamp of the Lord, searching all our inward parts. This shows that within man there is something of God, and this is man's spirit to be God's lamp. Of course, in the lamp is the light, so here the implication is very meaningful. Within man there is such a lamp, but the lamp needs the light, and the light is God. What man has is just an empty lamp. The lamp needs the light to shine. This shows that God as the light has something in man as His vessel to contain Him and to express Him, just as the lamp contains the light and expresses it.

The second point we have to stress is that this lamp of God, which is our spirit, searches all our inward parts. No doubt, this is altogether the inward searching, not the outward rebuking or instruction. We should help the saints realize how significant the human spirit is. Proverbs 20:27 can be used to impress the saints so that they can see how man's spirit is so close to God and is something of God within man. This is a strong point. The human spirit is God's vessel to contain God and to express God. Every lamp serves these two purposes. The lamp serves to contain the light and to express it. Then it works. When it works, it enlightens, it shines, and it searches.

II. OUR SPIRIT BEING THE HIDDEN MAN OF THE HEART

First Peter 3:4 reveals that our spirit is the hidden man of our heart. The hidden man is a meek and quiet spirit. When our spirit is meek and quiet, it is hidden. First Peter 3:4 indicates that every part of our being may be considered as a man. Our physical body is our outward man, our soul is our expressed, manifested man, and our spirit is our hidden man.

According to 1 Peter 3, the most beautiful part of our being, the prettiest adornment, in the sight of God is a meek and quiet spirit. This is the hidden man of the heart. This point shows that our spirit is the deepest part of our being. So if we are going to be pretty in the eyes of God, we have to be pretty from the depths of our being. We should not be pretty just outwardly, in a physical way. We have to be pretty inwardly, in the hidden man. This man is hidden from the eyes of man, but it is not hidden from the eyes of God, because such a hidden man, that is, a meek and quiet spirit, is pretty in the eyes of God.

We have to point out that 1 Peter 3:4, on the one hand, says something about the hidden man but, on the other hand, refers to it as being in the sight of God. This means that this meek and quiet spirit is hidden in our heart from human eyes, but it is not hidden in the sight of God. God sees it. So this is the real beauty that a godly person should have.

III. OUR REGENERATED SPIRIT
BEING OUR INNER MAN

We have to help the saints realize that our human spirit is the lamp of God, serving God with a purpose. Furthermore, this spirit is a beautiful, hidden man in the sight of God. Also, when our spirit is regenerated, it becomes the inner man (Eph. 3:16). The sense of the word *inner* is stronger than the sense of the word *hidden*. The hidden man is one that is not manifested, but the inner man can be very active and aggressive. According to Ephesians 3, the inner man must be very active and very aggressive to live the Lord out. After the inner man is strengthened, Christ has the way to make His home in our heart. This indicates that the inner man is not just something hidden, meek, and quiet but is something very living, active, and aggressive so that Christ may use it for Himself to make His home in our heart.

According to the Bible, I believe the above three points are the basic description of what our spirit is. Our spirit is the lamp of the Lord, a pretty, hidden man in God's eyes, and the inner man, living, active, and aggressive for the Lord to fulfill His purpose. These three points help us to know what our spirit is.

IV. OUR SPIRIT NEEDING TO BE STIRRED UP

Beginning from this point, we need to see what our spirit should do. Ezra 1:1 says that the Lord stirred up the spirit of Cyrus, king of Persia. Then verse 5 says that God stirred up the spirit of a remnant of Israelites to go up to build His house in Jerusalem. Our spirit needs to be stirred up for God's interest (cf. Exo. 35:21). We should not wait for others to stir up our spirit. Instead, we should stir up our spirit by exercising our spirit (cf. 2 Tim. 1:6-7). On the one hand, the Lord is the One who stirs our spirit up, but we should not be passive. We ourselves have to cooperate with the Lord to stir up our spirit.

V. OUR SPIRIT NEEDING TO BE BURNING

Our spirit needs to be burning. Romans 12:11 charges us to be burning in spirit, and Acts 18:25 tells us that Apollos was fervent, burning, in spirit.

VI. OUR SPIRIT INDWELT BY THE HOLY SPIRIT NEEDING TO BE THE FACULTY OF OUR PRAYER

Prayer is the way to exercise our spirit, but many Christians do not pray with their spirit. They pray by using merely their mouth and their mentality with their emotion. They do not use their spirit when they pray. If one person asks another person to do something for him, he might simply open up his mouth according to his mentality and his emotion without exercising his spirit. Many Christians today pray to the Lord in exactly the same way. They do not use their spirit.

In the past we prayed many times without exercising our spirit, but Ephesians 6:18 says that we need to pray at every time in our spirit. We need to use our spirit as the faculty of prayer. We cannot hear things by exercising our eyes or smell things by using our ears. We must use the proper faculty to hear and to smell. In the same way, we have to pray by exercising our spirit as the proper faculty of our prayer. The faculty for us to pray is not our mind or emotion but our spirit. The more we stress this, the better. Many saints and young ones among us need to learn how to use their spirit in prayer.

A good illustration of using the spirit is when a person loses his temper. When he loses his temper and yells, he is not using his mind. At that point, he is in his real person, that is, his spirit. If we do not yell from our spirit, our yelling is a false performance. The real yelling surely comes out of our spirit. Of course, this is a negative example, because when one loses his temper, his spirit comes forth in a cruel and rude way. But in principle, we have to learn to use our spirit in prayer in the same way. Whenever we open up our mouth, we should exercise our spirit to utter something. Whenever we pray, we should pray in our spirit, using our spirit to say something to the Lord. Our spirit indwelt by the Holy Spirit needs to be the faculty of our prayer.

VII. OUR SPIRIT NEEDING TO BE THE MEANS OF OUR WORSHIP

According to John 4:24, our spirit needs to be the means of our worship. We need to worship God the Spirit in our spirit and with our spirit. Many saints come to the meeting to meet, but they do not come to worship. We may go through the formality of meeting without rendering the Lord the real worship that He desires. To worship is to exercise our spirit. Whenever we begin to exercise our spirit, the worship begins. We may think that our worship begins when we call a hymn or when we pray. But our worship actually begins when our spirit rises up and is exercised.

In other words, in a meeting we may sing a lot of hymns, yet without worship. Even we may read many verses of the Bible, yet without worship. We may even pray without worship. Many so-called Christian services have singing, the reading of the Bible, a sermon, and a benediction, all without the exercise of the spirit. There is no worship because no one exercises his spirit.

Our meetings need to be full of the exercise of the spirit. When we come together to meet, before singing, before praying, before reading, before doing anything, all of us should exercise our spirit. There should be such a worshipping spirit in all our meetings. Many times the elders exercise their spirit to open the meeting. Then they stir up others' spirit. This is not the best situation. All the saints must rise up to exercise their spirit. We have to help the saints to realize that we need to use our spirit to worship. Our spirit needs to worship God directly apart from merely depending upon singing, reading, or praying in a formal way.

VIII. OUR SPIRIT NEEDING TO TAKE THE LEAD IN ENJOYING THE LORD

Our spirit needs to take the lead in enjoying the Lord. This is fully shown in Luke 1:46-47. In these verses Mary said, "My soul magnifies the Lord, and my spirit has exulted in God my Savior." These two verses, no doubt, are describing the enjoyment of the Lord, and in the enjoyment of the Lord, our spirit has to take the lead. First, Mary's spirit exulted in God; then her soul magnified the Lord. Her praise to God issued from her spirit and was expressed through her soul. But today we mostly use our soul first. We must learn to directly use our spirit and let the soul be a follower of the spirit. Our spirit must take the lead aggressively in enjoying the Lord. Our spirit should subdue our soul to make the soul its follower.

IX. OUR SPIRIT NEEDING TO TAKE THE INITIATIVE IN SPIRITUAL MINISTRY

First Corinthians 14:32 says, "The spirits of prophets are subject to prophets." In our spiritual ministry our spirit has to take the initiative. If our spirit is waiting, that means our spirit is dormant. On all occasions our spirit should take the initiative to minister something.

X. OUR SPIRIT KNOWING THE THINGS OF A MAN

To know the things of a man, we cannot depend upon our mind. To know a man, we need our spirit. First Corinthians 2:11a says that only the spirit of man can know the things of a man. If we do not know how to exercise our spirit, we cannot know people. To know people, we have to exercise our spirit. A person may come to us and speak something to us, but if we merely understand him with our mind according to his word, we will be cheated. We have to exercise our spirit to know his spirit and his intention behind his word.

XI. PERCEIVING THINGS IN OUR SPIRIT

We also need to perceive things in our spirit (Mark 2:8a, KJV). To observe things according to our sight and understanding is not the real perceiving. The proper perceiving is to see through things and to know things thoroughly by exercising our spirit.

XII. PURPOSING IN OUR SPIRIT

Paul purposed in his spirit (Acts 19:21a). We may think that to purpose or make a decision is always by using our will. But we must purpose and make decisions in our spirit. Then we are spiritual men.

XIII. JUDGING A PERSON IN OUR SPIRIT

First Corinthians 5 tells us that Paul judged a sinful one in the church in Corinth in his spirit (vv. 3-5a). We should not judge anyone superficially according to our feeling or understanding. We have to judge people in our spirit.

XIV. BEING A PERSON IN OUR SPIRIT

We need to be a person in our spirit. John says that he was in spirit on the Lord's Day (Rev. 1:10). To be a person in our spirit needs much exercise.

XV. EXERCISING OUR SPIRIT BY DOING THE ABOVEMENTIONED THINGS

To exercise our spirit we have to do all the abovementioned things.

THE EXERCISE OF OUR SPIRIT
FOR GODLINESS

Scripture Reading: 1 Tim. 1:3-4; 3:15-16; 4:7-8; 6:11; 2 Tim. 3:12, 5; 4:22; 2:22

OUTLINE

I. God's economy—1 Tim. 1:3-4.

II. The mystery of godliness—3:15-16:
  A. God manifested in the flesh.
  B. The church of the living God.

III. Exercising ourselves unto godliness—4:7-8:
  A. Bodily exercise profiting for a little.
  B. Godliness being profitable for all things:
    1. Of the present life.
    2. Of the coming life.

IV. Pursuing godliness to be a man of God—6:11.

V. Living godly in Christ—2 Tim. 3:12.

VI. Having the power of godliness—v. 5.

VII. The Lord being with our spirit—4:22:
  A. Contacting the Lord by exercising our spirit.
  B. Thus receiving grace.

VIII. Calling on the Lord—2:22:
  A. Out of a pure heart.
  B. With the Lord's callers.

In this lesson we want to see the exercise of our spirit for godliness. All the verses in the Scripture Reading are from 1 and 2 Timothy. Strictly speaking, the word *exercise,* in the sense of the exercise of our spirit for godliness, is used in the New Testament only in 1 Timothy. First Timothy 4:7-8 says, "The profane and old-womanish myths refuse, and exercise yourself unto godliness. For bodily exercise is profitable for a little, but godliness is profitable for all things, having promise of the present life and of that which is to come." The exercise unto godliness is profitable for all the things of this present life and the coming life.

In the New Testament there are a number of seeming contradictions. Actually, of course, they are not contradictions. On the one hand, the New Testament reveals that we should not have our own works. We should not do things in ourselves either to participate in God's blessing or to accomplish something for God's purpose. But on the other hand, the New Testament uses a strong word such as *exercise.* In Colossians Paul says that he labored, toiled, fought, and struggled in an agonizing way (1:29; 2:1). These words are stronger words showing something that is very difficult to do. We all need to see these two aspects. Our not doing anything means that we should not do anything by our flesh, by ourselves, or by our natural life. But on the positive side we have to labor, to travail, and to struggle in our spirit. Actually, the exercise of our spirit comprises and implies all these words: *labor, toil, struggle, wrestle,* and *fight.*

Today whatever we do positively in our spirit is a kind of exercise. The word in Greek for *exercise* is the basis of the English word *gymnastics.* To participate in gymnastics, one must use all his energy to exercise his whole physical being. We must exercise our spirit in the same way. The whole environment around us does not help us to exercise. It has an intention to keep us down. The whole situation does not help us to go on to labor. It helps us to be lazy; it helps us to be backsliding. It is a downhill current. The downhill current helps us go down. Actually, the current carries you. But if you go uphill, you have to exercise, and you have to struggle.

In this lesson we have extracted the life essence from 1 and

2 Timothy. These two books actually deal with godliness as the issue of the divine dispensing for the divine economy. In this lesson I did my best to pick up all the necessary verses to show us the life of godliness.

I. GOD'S ECONOMY

First Timothy 1:3 and 4 say, "Even as I exhorted you, when I was going into Macedonia, to remain in Ephesus in order that you might charge certain ones not to teach different things nor to give heed to myths and unending genealogies, which produce questionings rather than God's economy, which is in faith." These two verses indicate that 1 Timothy is dealing with God's economy. At Paul's time some were teaching different things other than God's economy. Paul told us that we have to put all these different teachings aside and come back to the economy of God. God's economy is His household administration, His plan, to dispense Himself into us. His dispensing produces a life of godliness. Actually, godliness is the issue of the divine dispensing.

Such a godly life issuing from God's dispensing depends upon the exercise of our spirit. The whole book of 1 Timothy shows us this. A godly life comes out of God's dispensing, but God is not dispensing Himself into lifeless vessels. In England they call a drugstore a dispensary. In the dispensary, drugs are dispensed into lifeless bottles, and because they are lifeless, their cooperation is not required. God, however, is dispensing Himself into us, the living vessels, who already have our own taste, choice, preference, feeling, thinking, mentality, will, etc. If we do not exercise our spirit strongly to cooperate with the Lord, God cannot dispense Himself into us. Our spirit is not only the receiving organ, the retaining organ, but also the opening for God's dispensing. When our spirit opens wide, our whole being opens. Then God has a way to impart Himself into us. God's dispensing depends upon our coordination, and our coordination is the exercise of our spirit.

This is why we have to pray. Just as walking exercises our feet and legs, only prayer exercises our spirit. When we pray, we should not be concerned so much for material things and for our personal affairs as the goal. We should pray in the spirit in order to touch God, to contact God, and to worship God. This kind of prayer exercises our spirit and opens our spirit, and in our spirit we meet God. Then the divine dispensing immediately flows into our spirit. Today our Christian life is a life of godliness, which comes out of God's dispensing of Himself into us. This depends upon our spirit being fully exercised.

II. THE MYSTERY OF GODLINESS

A. God Manifested in the Flesh

The mystery of godliness is God manifested in the flesh (3:15-16). Today we are the flesh in which God can be manifested. God is manifested in the flesh, but you have to realize that God can never be manifested *by* the flesh. The flesh is just the earthen vessel. It is not the key to carry out God's manifestation. The key of God's manifestation in us is our spirit.

B. The Church of the Living God

The church of the living God is the ultimate mystery of godliness because the proper church life is the corporate manifestation of God in the flesh. In order to usher all the saints into the proper exercise of our spirit, we have to point out all these basic points. We have to develop these points and impress the saints with them.

III. EXERCISING OURSELVES UNTO GODLINESS

First Timothy charges us to exercise ourselves unto godliness (4:7-8). Godliness is a Christian life, a godly life, that expresses God as the issue of God's dispensing, and this is a mystery. This godly life needs our exercise.

A. Bodily Exercise Profiting for a Little

Paul says that bodily exercise is profitable for a little. Bodily exercise profits for a few things and only for a small part of our being. Furthermore, this implies that it profits temporarily, for a little while. The word *bodily* indicates that the exercise unto godliness must be the exercise of our spirit. Paul points out that the exercise to which he is referring is not the exercise of the body. Surely he would not exhort us to exercise our soul. The exercise to which he is referring must be the exercise of our spirit. Even he says that you need to exercise yourself. "Yourself" is not the self in the body or in the soul; it must be the being in your spirit.

B. Godliness Being Profitable for All Things

Paul says that "godliness is profitable for all things" (v. 8). Godliness here is actually the exercise of our spirit. This is not an apparent revelation but an implied revelation. Paul says that bodily exercise profits for a little, but godliness profits for all things. This godliness must be the exercise of our spirit, which, in contrast to bodily exercise, is profitable for all things. *For all things* refers to things that are not only of one part of our being but of all parts—physical, psychological, and spiritual, both temporal and eternal.

1. Of the Present Life

The promise of the present life, a life that is in this age, is like the promises in Matthew 6:33, John 16:33, Philippians 4:6-7, and 1 Peter 5:8-10. *The present life* in 1 Timothy 4:8 does not mean our physical life, because the word here is *zoe,* referring to the divine, uncreated life of God. We have zoe in this present age. The exercise of our spirit, which carries out godliness, is profitable for all things, carrying with it the promise of the present divine life, which we have received and which we are enjoying.

2. Of the Coming Life

The promise of the coming life, a life that is in the next age and in eternity, is like the promises in 2 Peter 1:10-11; 2 Timothy 2:12; Revelation 2:7, 17; 21:6-7, etc. Godliness is profitable for all things of the present life and also of the coming life, referring to our spiritual life, not our physical life or soulish life.

IV. PURSUING GODLINESS TO BE A MAN OF GOD

Paul told Timothy, "You, O man of God, flee these things, and pursue righteousness, godliness, faith, love, endurance, meekness" (1 Tim. 6:11). Among these many items that Timothy was to pursue, the central item is godliness. We need to pursue godliness to be a man of God. Actually, godliness is just "Godlikeness." To be godly means to be like God, to express God. In other words, godliness is to live God out. Someone who lives God out is a man of God. Because he lives God out, he is like God. He bears God's likeness, so he is a man of God. A man of God has to pursue, to seek after, God-likeness.

V. LIVING GODLY IN CHRIST

Second Timothy 3:12 speaks of those who "desire to live godly in Christ Jesus." To live godly means that our life must be a godly life. Godliness must be our living, and this again depends upon the exercise of our spirit.

VI. HAVING THE POWER OF GODLINESS

Second Timothy 3:5 speaks of the power of godliness. Paul says that in the degradation of the church, some only have the outward form of godliness, but they do not have the power. The power must be by the exercise of our spirit. Some religious people may have ordinances about how to dress in an outward form of godliness, but there is no inward power with them. We have to exercise our spirit in all the things in our daily life so that we have the power of godliness. When we exercise our spirit, what we do is not a mere outward performance or form but a display of the genuine godliness with the inward power. This power, which comes from the inner exercise of our spirit, is the real and practical virtue with a living influence to express God.

VII. THE LORD BEING WITH OUR SPIRIT

At the end of 2 Timothy, Paul says, "The Lord be with your spirit" (4:22). The conclusion of this book emphasizes the Lord's being with our spirit.

A. Contacting the Lord by Exercising Our Spirit

The Lord is with our spirit, but we have to respond, to cooperate, by exercising our spirit. The air is with us, but we have to breathe in the air to enjoy it. The air can be enjoyed by us continuously because we have a breathing organ to get the benefit of the air. In the same way, the Lord, the Spirit, is with us, but we need to exercise our spirit, our breathing organ, to breathe in the Lord as our spiritual air (John 20:22). If our spirit is not exercised, we cannot receive His benefit. The Lord being with our spirit surely implies the exercise of our spirit.

B. Thus Receiving Grace

In 2 Timothy 4:22 there are two sentences. First, Paul says, "The Lord be with your spirit." Then he says, "Grace be with you." If we exercise our spirit to contact the Lord, to breathe Him in, we receive grace to stand against the downward current of the church's decline and carry out God's economy. Grace is the Lord received, enjoyed, and experienced by us. Second Timothy 4:22 speaks of a subjective matter, not of an objective benediction. The Lord's being with our spirit is something for us to experience by the exercise of our spirit.

VIII. CALLING ON THE LORD

In 2 Timothy 2:22 Paul charged Timothy to flee youthful lusts and pursue righteousness, faith, love, and peace with those who call on the Lord out of a pure heart. This indicates that the Lord's seekers must be His callers.

A. Out of a Pure Heart

We call on the name of the Lord by our spirit, yet it must be out of a pure heart. Our heart must be pure. A pure heart is a heart with a pure motive, a pure intention, a pure purpose, a pure will, a pure decision, a pure sensation, a pure feeling, and a pure thought. If these things are not pure, our heart is not pure. Thus, we cannot call on the Lord out of a pure heart. A pure heart is a heart seeking only God. The only goal of a pure heart is God Himself (Matt. 5:8). If we seek after anything other than God, our motive is not pure, and thus our heart is not pure. We must call on the Lord with an exercised spirit out of a pure heart. Our heart must be purified, and the heart includes all these things: motive, intention, purpose, will, decision, sensation, feeling, and thought. The heart must be pure in all its constituents. Then we can call on the Lord purely.

B. With the Lord's Callers

Second Timothy 2:22 implies that we need to call on the Lord with the Lord's callers. Sometimes we call on the Lord just by ourselves. This exercises our spirit, and we receive more of the Lord but not as much as when we call with some others. To have a corporate calling on the Lord helps a lot. In order to exercise our spirit, we have to recover the practice of calling on the name of the Lord. We need to exercise our spirit so that we may receive the Lord more. Then we can live a godly life to manifest God.

A PROPER SPIRIT

Scripture Reading: Psa. 51:10b, 12b, 17a; Isa. 57:15; 66:2; 1 Pet. 3:4; Gal. 6:1; 1 Cor. 4:21; Matt. 5:3; Luke 9:55

OUTLINE

I. A right spirit—Psa. 51:10b.

II. A willing spirit—v. 12b.

III. A broken spirit—v. 17a.

IV. A contrite and lowly spirit—Isa. 57:15; 66:2.

V. A meek and quiet spirit—1 Pet. 3:4; Gal. 6:1; 1 Cor. 4:21.

VI. Being poor in spirit—Matt. 5:3.

VII. Knowing of what spirit we are—Luke 9:55.

In the previous lesson we saw that we need to exercise our spirit for godliness. Now we want to see that we need to have a proper spirit.

I. A RIGHT SPIRIT

First, we need to have a right spirit (Psa. 51:10b, KJV). This does not refer to our spirit being right versus being wrong. A right spirit is an upright spirit. This means that it can stand as something constant. Some versions say that this is a steadfast, constant, or firm spirit. A right spirit is a spirit that is immovable, unshakable, standing constantly as something firm and steady.

Psalm 51 is the psalm of David for his repentance. He repented that his spirit was not right. In other words, his spirit did not stand upright constantly. His spirit was not steady, not firm, so he was able to be seduced, or tempted, and he fell. In his repentance he prayed that the Lord would renew a right spirit within him, a constant, firm, steady spirit. In his prayer for restoration he asked the Lord to renew such a spirit within him. We always need a right spirit, which is always steadfast, firm, constant, immovable, and unshakable so that we can never be tempted, seduced, or misled.

II. A WILLING SPIRIT

Also in Psalm 51 in David's repentance and confession, he prayed that God would give him a willing spirit (v. 12). David connected the willing spirit with the gladness of salvation. He asked the Lord to restore to him the gladness of salvation and sustain him with a willing spirit. A willing spirit depends upon the gladness of salvation. When we have the gladness of salvation, we spontaneously will have a willing spirit to go along with the Lord. We will have a willing spirit to answer, to obey, what the Lord wants, what the Lord desires, and what the Lord asks of us. This willing spirit always comes from our rejoicing in our salvation. We need the gladness of salvation.

No doubt, in David's fall he lost the gladness of his salvation. Now he was repenting, so he asked that God would restore to him the gladness of salvation. This means that God would bring him back to the enjoyment of salvation. Then from this enjoyment and this joy, he could have a willing spirit. A willing spirit is an issue of being happy and joyful in the Lord. Romans 14:17 says, "The kingdom of God is...righteousness and peace and joy in the Holy Spirit." When we have joy in God's Spirit, our spirit will be willing. We will have a willing spirit to fellowship with the Lord, to worship Him, and to pray. Whatever can please the Lord, we will be happy to do. This means that we have a willing spirit.

III. A BROKEN SPIRIT

In Psalm 51:17a David says that the sacrifices of God are a broken spirit. In other words, in God's eyes a broken spirit is more precious than sacrifices. In the second part of verse 17 David says that God will not despise a broken and a contrite heart. A broken spirit is a spirit that repents, that feels very sorrowful for any sinfulness. In other words, a broken spirit is a repenting spirit.

To be broken means to not be whole. Here it does not mean to be broken into pieces. It means that you do not consider yourself so perfect or complete. If you consider that you are perfect and complete, you would not repent or confess your weaknesses and your failures. When your spirit is repenting, your spirit is broken, contrite, and feeling sorrowful. After sinning, many would not have a broken spirit. Instead, they would have a spirit that is stubbornly whole. Because they feel that they are perfect and complete, they would not repent. They would not confess. We should not be like this. We should have a spirit that is always broken.

Even if we do not feel that we have sinned, we still need a broken spirit. Even if we have not sinned in a great way, we still could be wrong in a small way. In our words, our attitude, our thoughts, our feelings, and our talk with others, many times we are wrong, even unconsciously. So we always need to keep a broken spirit. Do not consider yourself as being whole, complete, and perfect. No one is perfect, so we always need a broken spirit to repent and confess.

IV. A CONTRITE AND LOWLY SPIRIT

A contrite and lowly spirit is very close to a broken spirit.

Isaiah 57:15 and 66:2 both indicate the same thing. They indicate that even heaven is not a joyful place to God for His dwelling. God desires to dwell with people who have a contrite and lowly spirit. This is not a small thing. If we are contrite and lowly in our spirit, we are broken in our spirit, and we can enjoy God's presence. God is then with us and even dwells with us.

If our spirit is proud and we keep ourselves complete, perfect, and whole, being unwilling to repent and confess, we will lose the Lord's presence. In a certain sense, according to our experience, the Lord's presence will leave us. So we need a contrite spirit, which is lowly and broken, a repenting spirit to confess our sinfulness. If we are in this kind of spirit, the Lord will be with us and will dwell with us. Isaiah 57:15 and 66:2 are wonderful verses to point out to the saints.

V. A MEEK AND QUIET SPIRIT

We also need a meek and quiet spirit. First Peter 3:4 says that the hidden man of our heart is a meek and quiet spirit. Galatians 6:1 says that we need to restore a fallen brother in a spirit of meekness. In 1 Corinthians 4:21 Paul asked the Corinthians if they wanted him to come to them with a rod or in love and in a spirit of meekness.

The New Testament mentions the virtue of meekness a number of times. In Matthew 5:5 the Lord said, "Blessed are the meek, for they shall inherit the earth." Based upon this verse we can look into the real meaning of being meek in the New Testament. The world's way is to fight, to strive, and to defeat others to gain some possession, some inheritance. But the Bible says that if we are going to inherit anything, we have to be meek. To be meek means not to resist the world's opposition but to suffer it willingly. Regardless of the situation we should be meek, not fighting against others. Meekness means not fighting for ourself. We need a meek and quiet spirit. If we fight for anything, we cannot be quiet. The only way that we can be quiet is to not fight for ourself or seek anything for ourself.

VI. BEING POOR IN SPIRIT

In Matthew 5:3 the Lord said, "Blessed are the poor in spirit, for theirs is the kingdom of the heavens." We may say that we need to have a rich spirit, but we should not say that we need to have a poor spirit. This is wrong. If someone has a poor spirit, his spirit is not a right spirit, a proper spirit. Here in Matthew 5:3 to be poor *in* spirit means that we have nothing preoccupying us. All the Pharisees, the scribes, the priests, and the elders among the Jewish people were not poor in spirit. They were preoccupied. That was the reason the Lord Jesus said that the first blessing is to be poor in spirit. The Pharisees could not participate in the kingdom because they were not poor in their spirit. We always need to be poor in our spirit, not letting our spirit be preoccupied, filled up, with things other than the Lord Himself. We have to empty our spirit, to pour out all the preoccupying items, so that we may be poor in our spirit.

VII. KNOWING OF WHAT SPIRIT WE ARE

Luke 9 tells us that a certain village of the Samaritans would not receive the Lord and His disciples. So James and John said, "Lord, do You want us to command fire to come down from heaven and consume them?" (v. 54). The Lord turned and rebuked them, saying, "You do not know of what kind of spirit you are" (v. 55). We always have to learn to know what kind of spirit we have. In other words, with God and with man we always need a proper spirit. If our spirit is improper, we are through with God. We need to know what condition our spirit is in. The Bible tells us to consider our ways (Hag. 1:7), and we also have to consider our spirit. We should consider not only our outward ways, our outward behavior, and our outward attitude but also our inward spirit. We need a proper spirit.

DISCERNING THE SPIRIT FROM THE SOUL

Scripture Reading: Heb. 4:12; Matt. 16:24, 26; Luke 9:25; Rom. 8:6b, 4; 1 Cor. 6:17

OUTLINE

I. The spirit being concealed in the soul just as the marrow is concealed in the joints—Heb. 4:12.

II. The soul needing to be broken so that the spirit may be divided from it just as the joints need to be broken so that the marrow may be divided from them.

III. The composition of the soul—the mind, emotion, and will—needing to be denied.

IV. The denial of the mind, emotion, and will being the denial of the self—Matt. 16:24, 26; Luke 9:25.

V. The living and operative word of God exposing and discerning the thoughts of the mind, the intentions of the will, and the desires of the emotion—Heb. 4:12.

VI. After the breaking of the soul—the denial of the mind, emotion, and will—whatever is left being the spirit.

VII. Setting the mind on the spirit—Rom. 8:6b.

VIII. Walking according to the spirit—v. 4.

IX. Being one with the Lord in the spirit—1 Cor. 6:17.

In this lesson we need to point out to the saints how to discern the spirit from the soul.

I. THE SPIRIT BEING CONCEALED IN THE SOUL
JUST AS THE MARROW IS CONCEALED IN THE JOINTS

Hebrews 4:12 shows that the spirit is concealed in the soul just as the marrow is concealed in the joints. Our spirit is like the marrow, and our soul is like the joints. In other words, our spirit is altogether wrapped up, enveloped, in our soul. The soul is the envelope that hides our spirit. So to discern our spirit from our soul, we must know where our spirit is. It is within our soul. Here we can also see the situation of our spirit. Our spirit is surrounded, enclosed, by our soul. To discern our spirit from our soul, we need to see the position and situation of our spirit.

II. THE SOUL NEEDING TO BE BROKEN
SO THAT THE SPIRIT MAY BE DIVIDED FROM IT
JUST AS THE JOINTS NEED TO BE BROKEN
SO THAT THE MARROW MAY BE DIVIDED FROM THEM

If the joints are not broken but are whole, the marrow can never be divided from the joints. In order to divide the marrow from the joints, we have to break the joints. This shows that without our soul being broken, our spirit can never be separated from our soul. In order for the contents to be divided from its cover, its wrapping, the cover must be broken. This is basic. Our soul must be broken. If we let our soul remain whole, there is no possibility for our spirit to be divided from it. To discern the spirit means not only to realize the difference between the spirit and the soul but also to divide the spirit from the soul. Thus, there is the need of the breaking of the soul.

III. THE COMPOSITION OF THE SOUL—
THE MIND, EMOTION, AND WILL—
NEEDING TO BE DENIED

The soul is composed of the mind, emotion, and will. All these components of the soul need to be denied. We should not give any ground to our mind, our emotion, or our will. They all have to be denied in our spiritual life.

IV. THE DENIAL OF THE MIND, EMOTION, AND WILL BEING THE DENIAL OF THE SELF

To deny our mind, emotion, and will is to deny ourselves. In Matthew 16:24 the Lord Jesus told us that to follow Him we need to deny ourselves. Matthew 16:26 compared with Luke 9:25 shows that our soul, our soulish life, is our self. The soul is the self. Thus, to deny the contents of the soul—the mind, emotion, and will—is to deny the self. Here we have to see that the denial is the breaking. To deny the mind, emotion, and will of our soul is to let the soul be broken. The real breaking of the soul is the denial of the self.

V. THE LIVING AND OPERATIVE WORD OF GOD EXPOSING AND DISCERNING THE THOUGHTS OF THE MIND, THE INTENTIONS OF THE WILL, AND THE DESIRES OF THE EMOTION

By the context of Hebrews 4:12, we can see that the living and operative word of God exposes and discerns the thoughts of our mind, the intentions of our will, and the desires of our emotion. Because the word of God exposes our inner situation, it discerns our entire inner situation. This is because the word of God is living and operative. *Living* refers to the nature of God's word, and *operative* refers to the function of the word. The word itself is living, and it operates, functions.

All the saints, including the older ones, need to understand why Paul mentions the word of God for the dividing of our spirit from our soul. This is because every time God speaks to us, His word always exposes and discerns our inner situation. Hebrews 4:12 is mentioned based upon the fact that God spoke to the children of Israel, charging them to go on directly into the good land. What God spoke to them exposed their inner situation and made their inner situation clear to them.

The children of Israel were absolutely in their soul. They were considering how tall and strong the Canaanites were and how weak they were. The Canaanites were giants and big in number, and the children of Israel were small in number. The children of Israel were considering all these things and were afraid of the Canaanites. This consideration, this thinking, was in their soul. Then the word of God exposed and discerned this to show them that they were in their soul. They did not exercise their spirit like Joshua and Caleb did. Joshua and Caleb did not remain in their soul. The Bible says that they had a different spirit (Num. 14:24, 30). They were exercising their spirit, so they had the faith.

Paul compares the staggering Hebrew believers to the children of Israel in ancient times. To Paul's registration the Hebrew believers were staggering. They were not clear what to do— whether to remain in Judaism or to go on in the Christian life. They were in their soul, not in their spirit. So Paul spoke the word of God to them to expose their inner situation and to help them to discern that they were in the soul, not in the spirit.

By this we can see that every time we read the word in the Bible in a living way, the word always either requires or demands something of us. This demanding word, or requiring word, always exposes and discerns our inner situation so that we know whether we are in the soul or in the spirit. To discern our spirit, we need to receive the living word. The more we pray-read the Word, the more it becomes living to us. This living word shows us where we are, in the spirit or in the soul. It is by this that our soul is exposed and our spirit is discerned from our soul. The word of God always shows us our inner position and inner situation. If we are to discern the spirit from the soul, we cannot stay away from the living and operative word of God.

VI. AFTER THE BREAKING OF THE SOUL— THE DENIAL OF THE MIND, EMOTION, AND WILL— WHATEVER IS LEFT BEING THE SPIRIT

After the breaking of the soul—the denial of the mind, emotion, and will—whatever is left is the spirit. First, we have to see that the breaking of the soul equals the denial of the mind, emotion, and will. After this breaking, or this denial, surely we still have something left. If the unbelievers denied the mind, emotion, and will, nothing would be left. But the more we deny the mind, emotion, and will, the more our spirit will rise up and stand up. Some saints may ask how they can know the spirit. We need to tell them to let their soul be broken to the utter-most by denying their mind, emotion, and will. Then whatever is left is the spirit. This is the way to discern the spirit. The spirit is what is left over after the breaking and denial of the soul.

VII. SETTING THE MIND ON THE SPIRIT

In Romans 8:6b Paul charges us to set our mind on the spirit. We must have the soul broken first. We must deny the mind, emotion, and will. Then we can set the mind on the spirit. Otherwise, it is impossible for anyone to set the mind on the spirit. The soul must be broken, and the self must be denied, including the mind, emotion, and will. Then something is left over. Then we have the clear ground to set our mind on what is left over. That is the spirit.

VIII. WALKING ACCORDING TO THE SPIRIT

In Romans 8:4 Paul charges us to walk according to the spirit. If we do not have our soul broken, our mind, emotion, and will denied, and if we do not set our mind on the spirit as the leftover, we cannot walk according to the spirit. If we walk according to our mind, emotion, and will, this means that we walk according to our soul, according to our self, not according to our spirit. It must be after the breaking of the soul, after the denial of the mind, emotion, and will, and after the setting of the mind on the spirit, that we walk according to the spirit.

IX. BEING ONE WITH THE LORD IN THE SPIRIT

At this point, it is easy for us to go on with the Lord in the spirit. Here we need to use 1 Corinthians 6:17—"He who is joined to the Lord is one spirit."

If we do not know how to discern the spirit from the soul, this means that we do not allow the soul to be broken and the self to be denied. It is not until we have the soul broken, the self denied, that we have the clear ground to set our mind on the spirit. Then we can walk according to the spirit, and we can be one with the Lord in such a spirit, a spirit fully discerned from the soul. Then the spirit is not concealed in the soul but discerned from the soul, the broken soul.

ABOUT THE AUTHOR

Witness Lee was born in 1905 in northern China and raised in a Christian family. At age 19 he was fully captured for Christ and immediately consecrated himself to preach the gospel for the rest of his life. Early in his service, he met Watchman Nee, a renowned preacher, teacher, and writer. Witness Lee labored together with Watchman Nee under his direction. In 1934 Watchman Nee entrusted Witness Lee with the responsibility for his publication operation, called the Shanghai Gospel Bookroom.

Prior to the Communist takeover in 1949, Witness Lee was sent by Watchman Nee and his other co-workers to Taiwan to ensure that the things delivered to them by the Lord would not be lost. Watchman Nee instructed Witness Lee to continue the former's publishing operation abroad as the Taiwan Gospel Bookroom, which has been publicly recognized as the publisher of Watchman Nee's works outside China. Witness Lee's work in Taiwan manifested the Lord's abundant blessing. From a mere 350 believers, newly fled from the mainland, the churches in Taiwan grew to 20,000 in five years.

In 1962 Witness Lee felt led of the Lord to come to the United States, settling in California. During his 35 years of service in the U.S., he ministered in weekly meetings and weekend conferences, delivering several thousand spoken messages. Much of his speaking has since been published as over 400 titles. Many of these have been translated into over fourteen languages. He gave his last public conference in February 1997 at the age of 91.

He leaves behind a prolific presentation of the truth in the Bible. His major work, *Life-study of the Bible,* comprises over 25,000 pages of commentary on every book of the Bible from the perspective of the believers' enjoyment and experience of God's divine life in Christ through the Holy Spirit. Witness Lee was the chief editor of a new translation of the New Testament into Chinese called the Recovery Version and directed the translation of the same into English. The Recovery Version also appears in a number of other languages. He provided an extensive body of footnotes, outlines, and spiritual cross references. A radio broadcast of his messages can be heard on Christian radio stations in the United States. In 1965 Witness Lee founded Living Stream Ministry, a non-profit corporation, located in Anaheim, California, which officially presents his and Watchman Nee's ministry.

Witness Lee's ministry emphasizes the experience of Christ as life and the practical oneness of the believers as the Body of Christ. Stressing the importance of attending to both these matters, he led the churches under his care to grow in Christian life and function. He was unbending in his conviction that God's goal is not narrow sectarianism but the Body of Christ. In time, believers began to meet simply as the church in their localities in response to this conviction. In recent years a number of new churches have been raised up in Russia and in many eastern European countries.

OTHER BOOKS PUBLISHED BY
Living Stream Ministry

Titles by Witness Lee:

Abraham—Called by God	978-0-7363-0359-0
The Experience of Life	978-0-87083-417-2
The Knowledge of Life	978-0-87083-419-6
The Tree of Life	978-0-87083-300-7
The Economy of God	978-0-87083-415-8
The Divine Economy	978-0-87083-268-0
God's New Testament Economy	978-0-87083-199-7
The World Situation and God's Move	978-0-87083-092-1
Christ vs. Religion	978-0-87083-010-5
The All-inclusive Christ	978-0-87083-020-4
Gospel Outlines	978-0-87083-039-6
Character	978-0-87083-322-9
The Secret of Experiencing Christ	978-0-87083-227-7
The Life and Way for the Practice of the Church Life	978-0-87083-785-2
The Basic Revelation in the Holy Scriptures	978-0-87083-105-8
The Crucial Revelation of Life in the Scriptures	978-0-87083-372-4
The Spirit with Our Spirit	978-0-87083-798-2
Christ as the Reality	978-0-87083-047-1
The Central Line of the Divine Revelation	978-0-87083-960-3
The Full Knowledge of the Word of God	978-0-87083-289-5
Watchman Nee—A Seer of the Divine Revelation ...	978-0-87083-625-1

Titles by Watchman Nee:

How to Study the Bible	978-0-7363-0407-8
God's Overcomers	978-0-7363-0433-7
The New Covenant	978-0-7363-0088-9
The Spiritual Man • 3 volumes	978-0-7363-0269-2
Authority and Submission	978-0-7363-0185-5
The Overcoming Life	978-1-57593-817-2
The Glorious Church	978-0-87083-745-6
The Prayer Ministry of the Church	978-0-87083-860-6
The Breaking of the Outer Man and the Release ...	978-1-57593-955-1
The Mystery of Christ	978-1-57593-954-4
The God of Abraham, Isaac, and Jacob	978-0-87083-932-0
The Song of Songs	978-0-87083-872-9
The Gospel of God • 2 volumes	978-1-57593-953-7
The Normal Christian Church Life	978-0-87083-027-3
The Character of the Lord's Worker	978-1-57593-322-1
The Normal Christian Faith	978-0-87083-748-7
Watchman Nee's Testimony	978-0-87083-051-8

Available at
Christian bookstores, or contact Living Stream Ministry
2431 W. La Palma Ave. • Anaheim, CA 92801
1-800-549-5164 • www.livingstream.com